Deeds of the Hearts

Ibn Taymiyyah

Alreshah.net

Canada

Copyright © 2022 by **Alreshah**

All rights reserved. No part of this publication may be reproduced, distributed or transmitted in any form or by any means, without prior written permission.

Alreshah
www.Alreshah.net

Publisher's Note: This is a translation of a book without change of meaning as best as the translator could achieve with a few comments in the footnote to clarify If any error is found please contact us through our website alreshah.net.

Book Layout © 2017 BookDesignTemplates.com

Deeds of the Hearts / Ibn Taymiyyah. -- 1st ed.
ISBN 978-1-989875-22-3

The Book is translation of Ibn Taymiyyah's book .

Contents

Introduction 1

Deeds of the Bodies 3

The Danger of Novelty (Heresy, Badaa'ah) and its Impact upon Repentance 9

The Harm of Following Inclinations 13

Truth Necessitates Righteousness and it is the Root of the Religion 15

Truthfulness and belief in Words and Deeds 21

Sincerity is the Essence of Islam 23

Inward Deeds 27

    Such as Love, Sincerity, Reliance and Contentment And When Grief is Permitted or Forbidden 27

    The Essence of Reliance 30

    [The Meaning of Worshipping] 33

    [of Perfect and Utmost Love and Humility for Allah] 33

    Fate and Predestination 37

    The Classification of the Words, the Commands, the Will, the Permission, the Writing, the Decreeing, the Judgment and the Prohibition into Universal and Religious 41

His (PBUH) Description in the Torah 57

Refraining from Exposing Oneself to Trial............................65

Forbearance and its Provisions 67

Contentment and its Provisions 70

Of Perfect Contentment: Praise 74

The Marks of the Sincere Repentance 78

Love for Allah and His Messenger (PBUH)..........................83

Fear and Hope and Confuting those who Allege they Worship but not out of Longing to His Paradise or Fear of His Hellfire 105

Qur'anic Hearing and Satanic Hearing 127

Precious Words of Ubayy ibn Ka'ab (may Allah be pleased with him) 129

The Foundation of Love is Knowledge about Allah..............141

• CHAPTER 1 •

Introduction

In the Name of Allah, the All-Merciful, Most Merciful

All praise is due to Allah. We ask for His aid and forgiveness, and we seek His refuge from the evils of our-selves and from the ill of our deeds. For whoever Allah guides, there is no misleader; and for whoever Allah sends astray, there is no guide. We bear witness that there is no deity except Allah, alone and without a partner, and we bear witness that Muhammad (PBUH) is his servant and messenger.

These are brief words about the deeds of the hearts – which may be called "The Ranks and States" – which are among the foundations of faith and the bases of the religion, such as love for Allah and His Messenger, reliance upon Allah, sincerity of the religion for Him, gratitude for Him, endurance of His judgment, fear of Him, hope in Him and what follows that. This was asked [of me] by some of the people of faith whose rights were made obligatory by Allah, and they had them written; we are all hasty.

• CHAPTER 2 •

Deeds of the Bodies

I say: All of these deeds are obligatory for all creatures — who are originally responsible — as per the consensus of the imams of the religion. People, concerning them, are divided into three ranks, just as they are concerning the deeds of the bodies: (1) he who wrongs himself, (2) he who is moderate, and (3) he who is foremost in good deeds.

The one who wrongs himself: is the one who disobeys by disregarding a command or committing a forbidden deed.

The moderate: is the one who fulfils obligations and refrains from forbidden deeds.

The foremost in good deeds: is the one who seeks nearness [to Allah] by doing the obligatory [and optional] deeds within his capacity and refraining from forbidden and disapproved deeds. If the moderate and the foremost have sins, they are erased either **with repentance** – for Allah loves those who are constantly repentant and loves those who purify themselves, with erasing good deeds, with expatiating calamities or with something else.

Both the moderate and the foremost types are among the allies of Allah whom He mentioned in His book in His saying: "**{Unquestionably, [for] the allies of Allah there will be no fear concerning them, nor will they grieve - Those who believed and were fearing Allah.}**" [10:62-63]. The allies of Allah are the believers and god-fearing, but they are divided into "general public" who are the moderate and "select few" who are the foremost. The foremost are the highest in rank, such as the Prophets and the supporters of the truth.

The Prophet (PBUH) mentioned both types in the hadith stated by al-Bukhari in his "Sahih" from Abu Hurairah (may Allah be pleased with him) from the Prophet (PBUH) that he said: "**Allah said: "I will declare war against him who shows hostility to a pious worshipper of Mine. And the most beloved things with** *which My servant comes nearer to Me, is what I have enjoined upon him; and My servant keeps on coming closer to Me through performing Nawafil (non-obligatory good deeds) till I love him. When I love him, I become his sense of hearing with which he hears, and his sense of sight with which he sees, and his hand with which he grips, and his leg with which he walks; and if he asks Me, I will give him, and if he asks My protection, I will protect him; and I do not hesitate to do anything as I hesitate to take the soul of the believer, for he hates death, and I hate to disappoint him, but there is no escaping it."*"

As for the believer **who wrongs himself**: he has an alliance with Allah to the extent of his belief and piety, and he has of the opposite of that to the extent of his wickedness. The single person can exhibit reward-necessitating good deeds and punishment-necessitating bad deeds simultaneously, meaning that he can be rewarded and punished. This is the view of all the Messenger's (PBUH) companions, the Imams of Islam, and the People of the Sunnah and the Consensus who proclaim that anyone who has an atom's weight of faith in his heart shall not be sentenced to eternity in Hellfire.

As for those who purport Takhlid, such as al-Khawarij and al-Muʿtazila, who proclaim that any Muslim who enters Hellfire shall not leave it, and that there is no intercession for the Messenger (PBUH) or anyone else for the people of major sins, neither before nor after their entering Hellfire. In their view, reward and punishment, and good and bad deeds do not come together in the same person. Rather, whoever is rewarded shall not be punished, and whoever is punished shall not be rewarded. The evidence for that foundation from the Book, the Sunnah and the consensus of the early Muslim scholars is abundant, and this is not the place for it, as we have explained it in detail elsewhere.

Many things are based upon this. Therefore, he who has real faith must have of these deeds to the extent of his faith, even if he has sins.

Al-Bukhari stated in his Sahih that Umar ibn al-Khattab (may Allah be pleased with him) said: During the lifetime of the Prophet (PBUH) there was a man whose nickname was Donkey, and he used to make Allah's Messenger (PBUH) laugh. The Prophet (PBUH) lashed him because of drinking (alcohol). One day, he was brought to the Prophet (PBUH) on the same charge and a man among the people said: *"O Allah, curse him! How frequently he has been brought (to the Prophet (PBUH)) on such a charge)!"* The Prophet (PBUH) said, "**Do not curse him, for by Allah, I know for he loves Allah and His Apostle.**"

This clarifies that the sinner with drinking and whatnot may love Allah and His Messenger. The love of Allah and His Messenger is the strongest knot of faith. On the other hand, the ascetic worshipper, who has novelty and hypocrisy in his heart, may be resented by Allah and His Messenger for that aspect. It was numerously stated in the Sahih books[1], from that narrations of Amir al-Mu'minin Ali ibn abu Talib, Abu Saied al-Khudri and others that the Prophet (PBUH) spoke about al-Khawarij and said: "**There will appear some people among you whose prayer will make you look down upon yours, whose fasting will make you look down upon yours, and whose recitation will make you look down upon yours. But they will recite the Qur'an which will not exceed their throats (i.e., they will not act on it) and they will go out of Islam as an arrow goes out through the game. Whenever you face them, kill them, for killing them yields a reward by Allah for the one who kills them on the Day of Judgment. If I should live up to their time, I will kill them as the people of 'Ad were killed (i.e., I will kill all of them).**"

---

[1] This term refers to Sahih al-Bukhari and Sahih Muslim.

Those people were fought by the Messenger's (PBUH) companions with Amir al-Mu'minin Ali ibn abu Talib, as per the command of the Prophet (PBUH).

The Prophet (PBUH) said about them the authentic hadith: *"**A group would secede itself (from the Ummah) when there would be dissension among the Muslims. Out of the two groups who would be nearer the truth would kill them.**"*

CHAPTER 3

The Danger of Novelty (Heresy, Badaa'ah) and its Impact upon Repentance

This is why the Imams of Islam, such as Sufian al-Thawry and others, said that the novelty is dearer to Satan than the sin, because one does not repent from novelty but repents from sin.

The meaning of their saying that one does not repent from novelty is that for the committer of novelty, who takes a religion that was not ordained by Allah or His Messenger, the evil of his deed has been made attractive to him so he considers it good. Therefore, he does not repent as long as he considers it good, because the first step of repentance is realizing that he did an evil deed in order to repent from it, or that he neglected a good, obligatory or recommended, deed in order to repent and do it.

As long as he considers his deed good while it is bad, he will not repent.

However, repentance is possible if Allah guides him until the truth becomes clear to him, just as Allah guided whomever He guided of the infidels, the hypocrites, and the people of aberration and novelty. This results from following what he knows of the truth. Whoever puts what he knows into practice, Allah grants him knowledge of what he does not know, as He (the Exalted) said: "*{And those who are guided - He increases them in guidance and gives them their righteousness.}*" [47:17]. He (the Exalted) also said: "*{... But if they had done what they were instructed, it would have been better for them and a firmer position [for them in faith]. And then We would have given them from Us a great reward. And We would have guided them to a straight path.}*" [4:66-68].

He (The Exalted) also said: "*{O you who have believed, fear Allah and believe in His Messenger; He will [then] give you a* *double portion of His mercy and make for you a light by which you will walk and forgive you; and Allah is Forgiving and Merciful.}*" [57:28], He said: "*{Allah is the Ally of those who believe. He brings them out from darknesses into the light ...}*" [2:257], He said: "*{... There has come to you from Allah a light and a clear Book [i.e., the Qur'ān] By which Allah guides those who pursue His pleasure to the ways of peace and brings them out from darknesses into the light, by His permission, and guides them to a straight path.}*" [5:15-16]. The evidence for this concept is abundant in the Book and the Sunnah.

• CHAPTER 4 •

The Harm of Following Inclinations

On the other hand, whoever turns away from following what he knows to be true to follow his own inclinations, this grants him ignorance and aberration until heart is blinded from the clear truth. Allah (the Exalted) said: "*{And when they deviated, Allah caused their hearts to deviate. And Allah does not guide the defiantly disobedient people.}*" [61:5]. He (the Exalted) also said: "*{In their hearts is disease, so Allah has increased their disease …}*" [2:10]. He (the Exalted) also said: "*{And they swear by Allah their strongest oaths that if a sign came to them, they would surely believe in it. Say, "The signs are only with [i.e., from] Allah." And what will make you perceive that even if it* *[i.e., a sign] came, they would not believe. And We will turn away their hearts and their eyes just as they refused to believe in it [i.e., the revelation] the first time. And We will leave them in their transgression, wandering blindly.}"* [6:109-110]. This is an interrogative of negation and denial, i.e., how would you know that even if it came, they would not believe and that we turn away their hearts and eyes as they refused to believe in it the first time? According to a different recitation, it is a confirmation that even if it came, they would not believe and that we turn away their hearts and eyes as they refused to believe in it the first time. This is why some of the early scholars, such as **Saied ibn Jubair**, said: *"One of the rewards of a good deed is the subsequent good deed, and one of the punishments of a bad deed is the subsequent bad deed."*

• CHAPTER 5 •

Truth Necessitates Righteousness and it is the Root of the Religion

It was stated in the Sahihs that Ibn Mas'oud (may Allah be pleased with him) narrated that the Prophet (PBUH) said: *"Adhere to the truth, for truthfulness leads to righteousness, and righteousness leads to Paradise. And a man keeps on telling the truth until he is written before Allah as a truthful person. And beware falsehood, for falsehood leads to wickedness, and wickedness leads to Hellfire, and a man may keep on telling lies till he is written before Allah as a liar."* The

Prophet (PBUH) informed that truthfulness necessitates righteousness, and lying necessitates wickedness.

Allah (the Exalted) said: "*{Indeed, the righteous will be in pleasure, And indeed, the wicked will be in Hellfire.}*" [82:13-14]. That is why when some scholars wanted to command a follower of theirs to repent without repelling or overburdening him, they commanded him to be truthful.

This is why the mention of truthfulness and sincerity was frequent in the words of the Sheikhs and Imams of the religion, so much so that they said: *"Tell whoever is not truthful not to follow me."* They also said: *"Truthfulness is Allah's sword on earth; it was not put on something except it cut it."* **Yusuf ibn Asbat** and others said: *"No person is sincere to Allah except Allah grants him [above what He grants others],"* and many similar statements.

Truthfulness and sincerity are, in fact, the realization of Iman (faith) and Islam (submission). Those who exhibit Islam are divided into believers and hypocrites, and the difference between the believer and the hypocrite is sincerity. The basis upon which hypocrisy is built is falsehood. This is why when Allah mentions the essence of belief, it characterizes it as truthfulness, as He (the Exalted) said: "*{The Bedouins say, "We have believed." Say, "You have not [yet] believed; but say [instead], 'We have submitted,' ...}*" until His saying: "*{The believers are only the ones who have believed in Allah and His Messenger and then doubt not but strive with their properties and their lives in the cause of Allah. It is those who are the truthful.}*" [49:14-15].

He (the Exalted) also said: "*{For the poor emigrants who were expelled from their homes and their properties, seeking bounty from Allah and [His] approval and supporting [the cause of] Allah and His Messenger, [there is also a share]. Those are the truthful.}*" [59:8].

Thereupon, He stated that the truthful in the claim of faith are the believers whose belief was not followed by doubt, and who strived in His cause with their properties and their lives, as this is the covenant taken upon the formers and the latters, as He (the Exalted) said: "*{And [recall, O People of the Scripture], when Allah took the covenant of the prophets, [saying], "Whatever I give you of the Scripture and wisdom and then there comes to you a messenger confirming what is with you, you [must] believe in him and support him." [Allah] said, "Have you acknowledged and taken upon that My*

commitment?" They said, "We have acknowledged it." He said, "Then bear witness, and I am with you among the witnesses."} [3:81]. Ibn Abbas said: *"Allah did not send a prophet without taking his covenant that if Muhammad (PBUH) was sent during his lifetime, he would believe in him and support him, and commanding him to take the covenant of his followers that if Muhammad (PBUH) was sent during their lifetime, they would believe in him and support him."*

He (the Exalted) also said: "***{We have already sent Our messengers with clear evidences and sent down with them the Scripture and the balance that the people may maintain [their affairs] in justice. And We sent down iron, wherein is great military might and benefits for the people, and so that Allah may make evident those who support Him and His messengers unseen. Indeed, Allah is Powerful and Exalted in Might.}***" [57:25]. He (the Exalted) mentioned that He sent down the scripture and the balance, and that He sent down iron so that the people may maintain justice, and so that Allah may make evident those who support Him and His messengers. **This is why the backbones of the religion are a book that guides and a sword that supports**. But sufficient is your Lord as a guide and a helper.

Even if the scripture and the iron were both sent down, that does not prevent them from being sent down from different places. The scripture was sent down from Allah. as He (the Exalted) said: "*{The revelation of the Book [i.e., the Qur'ān] is from Allah, the Exalted in Might, the Wise.}*" [39:1], and said: "*{Alif, Lām, Rā. [This is] a Book whose verses are perfected and then presented in detail from [one who is] Wise and Aware}*" [11:1], and said: "*{And indeed, [O Muhammad], you receive the Qur'ān from one Wise and Knowing.}*" [27:6], while the iron was sent down from the mountains in which it was created.

In addition, He described the truthful in the call for righteousness, which is the root of the religion, in His saying: "*{Righteousness is not that you turn your faces toward the east or the west, but [true] righteousness is [in] one who believes in Allah, the Last Day, the angels, the Book, and the prophets ...}*" until He said: "*{... Those are the ones who have been true, and it is those who are the righteous.}*" [2:177]. As for the hypocrites, He (the Exalted) described them as liars in many verses, such as His saying: "*{In their hearts is disease, so Allah has increased their disease ...}*" [2:10], His saying: "*{When the hypocrites come to you, [O Muhammad], they* *say, "We testify that you are the Messenger of Allah." And Allah knows that you are His Messenger, and Allah testifies that the hypocrites are liars.}* " [63:1], and His saying: "*{So He penalized them with hypocrisy in their hearts until the Day they will meet Him - because they failed Allah in what they promised Him and because they [habitually] used to lie.}* " [9:77], and many other instances in the Holy Qur'an.

CHAPTER 6

Truthfulness and belief in Words and Deeds

One thing that should be known is that truthfulness and belief are in words and deeds, such as what the Prophet (PBUH) said in the authentic hadith: *"The very portion of Zina (adultery) in which a man will indulge was written. There will be no escape from it. The Zina of the eye is the (lustful) look, the Zina of the ears is the listening (to voluptuous songs or talk), the Zina of the hand is the (lustful) grip, the Zina of the feet is the walking (to the place where he intends to commit Zina), the heart yearns and desires and the private parts believe all that or disbelieves it."*

It is said: "They charged at the enemy sincerely," if their resolve for fighting was firm and unyielding.

It is said: "This person is of a sincere love, friendship and so on."

Thus, they characterize as truthful the sincere in his resolve, intention and pursuit, i.e., the sincere in his actions, and they also refer to the truthful in his speech and reports.

The hypocrite is the opposite of the sincere believer, which refers to the dishonest in his speech or insincere in his actions, such as the ostentatious.

Allah (the Exalted) said: "*{Indeed, the hypocrites [think to] deceive Allah, but He is deceiving them. And when they stand for prayer, they stand lazily, showing [themselves to] the people and not remembering Allah except a little.}*" until the end of the next verse [4:142-143].

CHAPTER 7

Sincerity is the Essence of Islam

Sincerity is the essence of Islam, for Islam is submission to Allah and no one else, as He (the Exalted) said: "*{Allah presents an example: a man [i.e., slave] owned by quarreling partners and another belonging exclusively to one man - are they equal in comparison? ...}*" until the end of the verse [39:29].

Whoever does not submit to Allah is arrogant, and whoever submits to Allah and others beside Him has committed polytheism. Both arrogance and polytheism are against Islam, and Islam (submission) is against polytheism and arrogance, and it [i.e., the verb to submit] is used both as a transitive and intransitive verb, as He (the Exalted) said: "*{When his Lord said* *to him, "Submit," he said, "I have submitted to the Lord of the worlds."}* [2:131], and said: *"{Yes, [on the contrary], whoever submits his face [i.e., self] in Islām to Allah while being a doer of good will have his reward with his Lord. And no fear will there be concerning them, nor will they grieve.}"* [2:112]. There are many such instances in the Holy Qur'an.

This is why the headline of Islam is "testifying that there is no deity except Allah", which includes worshipping Allah alone and renouncing the worshipping of anything else. This is the general Islam (submission) except which no other religion is accepted by Allah from the formers or the latters.

He (the Exalted) said: *"{And whoever desires other than Islām as religion - never will it be accepted from him, and he, in the Hereafter, will be among the losers.}"* [3:85], and said: *"{Allah witnesses that there is no deity except Him, and [so do] the angels and those of knowledge - [that He is] maintaining [creation] in justice. There is no deity except Him, the Exalted in Might, the Wise.}"* [3:18].

What we mentioned above clarifies that the foundation of the religion is in fact the inward affairs of knowledge and deeds, and that the outward deeds do not suffice without them. The

Prophet (PBUH) said in the hadith stated by Ahmad in his Musnad: *"**Islam is a public matter while Iman (faith) is in the heart.**"*

This is why the Prophet (PBUH) said in the hadith stated by al-Bukhari and Muslim, as narrated by al-Nu'man ibn Bashir, that the Prophet (PBUH) said: *"**What is lawful is clear and what is unlawful is clear, but between them are certain doubtful things which many people do not know. So, he who guards against doubtful things keeps his religion and his honor blameless. But he who falls into doubtful things falls into that which is unlawful, just as a shepherd who grazes his cattle in the vicinity of a pasture declared prohibited (by the king); he is likely to stray into the pasture. Mind you, every king has a protected pasture and Allah's involved limits is that which He has declared unlawful. Verily, there is a piece of flesh in the body, if it is healthy, the whole body is healthy, and if it is corrupt, the whole body is corrupt. Verily, it is the heart.**"* It is narrated that Abu Hurairah said: *"The heart is a king and the organs are his soldiers. If the king is good, his soldiers are good, and if the king is evil, his soldiers are evil."*

• CHAPTER 8 •

Inward Deeds

Such as Love, Sincerity, Reliance and Contentment
And When Grief is Permitted or Forbidden

These inward deeds, such as love for Allah, sincerity to Him, reliance upon Him, contentment with Him and so on, are all ordained for the general public and the select few, and leaving them is not praiseworthy for anyone, whatever his rank was.

As for **"grief"**, it was not commanded by Allah or His Messenger. Rather, it was forbidden in various instances, even if it was related to the affairs of the religion.

Such as His saying: "*{So do not weaken and do not grieve, and you will be superior if you are [true] believers.}*" [3:139].

As well as His saying: "*{... And do not grieve over them and do not be in distress over what they conspire.}*" [16:127], His saying: "*{... and he [i.e., Muhammad (PBUH)] said to his companion, "Do not grieve; indeed Allah is with us." ...}*" [9:40], His saying: "*{And let not their speech grieve you. ...}*" [10:65], and His saying: "*{In order that you not despair over what has eluded you and not exult [in pride] over what He has given you ...}*" [57:23], and many similar instances.

This is because it does not bring benefit or prevent harm, so it is pointless, and Allah does not command a pointless thing. Sure! The person who does it does not commit a sin as long as his grief is not accompanied by a forbidden deed, such as in the case of grief over calamities. The Prophet (PBUH) said: "**Allah does not punish for the shedding of tears or the grief of the heart, but takes to task or show mercy because of the utterances of this (and he pointed to his tongue)**". He (PBUH) also said: "**Our eyes shed tears and our hearts are filled with grief, but we do not say anything except that by which Allah is pleased.**" Another example is Allah's (the Exalted) saying: "*{And he turned away from them and said, "Oh, my sorrow*

over Joseph," and his eyes became white from grief, for he was [of that] a suppressor.}" [12:84].

Grief may be accompanied by something that rewards the person engaged in it, so it becomes praiseworthy from that aspect, rather than from the aspect of the grief itself, such as grief over a calamity in his religion and the calamities of Muslims in general. Such a person is rewarded for the love for good and the hate for evil that he has in his heart and what follows that. However, if such grief led to neglecting a commanded deed, such as forbearance, jihad, bringing a benefit or preventing a harm, it is prohibited. Otherwise, it suffices for the person to be relieved of the sin related to grief.

However, if it led to the weakness of the heart and its distraction with it from what Allah and His Messenger commanded, it is detested from that aspect, even if it were praiseworthy from other aspects.

As for love for Allah, reliance upon Him, sincerity to Him and so on, all these are purely good, and they are fine and desirable for every one of the prophets, the steadfast affirmers of truth, the martyrs and the righteous. Whoever proclaims that these ranks are for the general public and not the select few is mistaken if he meant to exclude the select few from them, for no believer is excluded from them. Rather, only the disbeliever or the hypocrite is excluded from them.

The Essence of Reliance

Some have made statements, in this regard, which we have shown to be wrong and falling short of achieving such ranks (in lengthy words), but this is not the right place for that.

However, concerning these "ranks", people are divided into general public and select few, and each have their own ranks.

An example for this is that they said: *"Reliance is a struggle on behalf of oneself in pursuing the living, while the select few do not struggle on behalf of themselves."* They also said: *"The relying person seeks, with his reliance, a certain matter, while the acquainted [with Allah] witnesses matters and their offshoots and seek none thereof."*

We respond: First of all, reliance is not restricted to worldly matters, for the relying person relies upon Allah concerning the uprightness of his heart and religion and the preservation of his tongue and will, which is the most important matter to him. That is why one confides in every prayer saying: "*{It is You we worship and You we ask for help.}*" [1:5], as in His saying: "*{... so worship Him and rely upon Him ...}*" [11:123], His saying: "*{... upon Him I have relied, and to Him I turn back.}*" [11:88], and His saying: "*{... Say, "He is my Lord; there is no deity except Him. Upon Him I rely, and to Him is my return."}*" [13:30].

Allah combined worshipping with reliance in multiple instances, because both of them contain the whole religion.

This is why some early scholar said: "*Allah combined the revealed books in the Holy Qur'an, combined the knowledge of the Qur'an in al-Mufassal[2], combined the knowledge of al-Mufassal in Surah al-Fatihah[3], and combined the knowledge of Surah al-Fatihah in His saying: "{It is You we worship and You we ask for help.}"*"

These two phrases are the comprehensive ones for the Lord and the servant, as in the hadith found in Sahih Muslim, from Abu Hurairah, that the Prophet (PBUH) said: "**Allah the Exalted**

---

[2] Al-Mufassal refers to the relatively shorter chapters of the Holy Qur'an, namely from Surah Qaf (Chapter 50) until the end of the Mus'haf.
[3] The 1st chapter of the Holy Qur'an.

had said: I have divided the prayer into two halves between Me and My servant, and My servant will receive what he asks. When the servant says: "{[All] praise is [due] to Allah, Lord of the worlds}", Allah the Most High says: "My servant has praised Me." And when he (the servant) says: "{The Entirely Merciful, the Especially Merciful}", Allah the Most High says: "My servant has lauded Me." And when he (the servant) says: "{Sovereign of the Day of Recompense}", He remarks: "My servant has glorified Me." And when he (the worshipper) says: "{It is You we worship and You we ask for help}", He (Allah) says: "This is between Me and My servant, and My servant will receive what he asks for." Then, when he (the worshipper) says: "{Guide us to the straight path - The path of those upon whom You have bestowed favor, not of those who have earned [Your] anger or of those who are astray}", He (Allah) says: This is for My servant, and My servant will receive what he asks for." The Lord (the Exalted) has the half of praise and goodness, and the servant has the half of prayer and request. These two phrases combine what is for the Lord (the Exalted) and what is for the servant: "**{It is You we worship}**" is for the Lord, while "**{and You we ask for help}**" is for the servant.

[The Meaning of Worshipping]

[of Perfect and Utmost Love and Humility for Allah]

It is stated in the Sahih books, that Mu'adh (may Allah be pleased with him) said: "*I was riding a pillion with the Prophet (PBUH) on a donkey, and he (PBUH) said:* **"O Mu'adh, do you know what is the right of Allah upon His servants?"** I said: "Allah and His Messenger know better." He said, **"Allah's Right upon His servants is that they should worship Him Alone and associate nothing with Him. Do you know what is the right of the servants upon Allah if they did so?"** I said: "Allah and His Messenger know better." He said: **"Their right upon Him is that He should not punish them.**"

Worshipping: is the end for which Allah created the servants, concerning Allah's command, love and pleasure. He (the Exalted) said: "*{And I did not create the jinn and mankind except to worship Me.}*" [51:56]. With it, the Messengers were sent and the Books were revealed. It is a name that combines perfect and utmost love for Allah with perfect and utmost humility for Allah. Love without humility and humility without love cannot be worshipping. Worshipping is the combination of the perfectness of both. Therefore, worshipping cannot be except for Allah, and even though its benefit is for the servant, and Allah is free from need of the worlds, it is for Allah from the aspect of His love for it and pleasure with it.

This is why Allah rejoices more with the servant's repentance than a man who lost his mount, which held his food and water, in a barren, dangerous land, and, after losing hope and going to sleep, he woke up to find it. Allah rejoices more with the repentance of His servant than this man with the return of his mount.

A number of significant matters, which we explained in detail elsewhere, are related to this.

Reliance and requesting help are for the servant, because they are the means and the path to attain his purpose and aim of worshipping. Calling for help is like supplication and beseeching. Al-Tabarani narrated in the book of "Do'aa (Prayer)" that the Prophet (PBUH) said: "**Allah (the Exalted, the Majestic) said: "O son of Adam! There are only four [that matter]; one for Me, one for you, one between Me and you and one between you and My creatures. As for the one that is for me, it is that you worship me and not associate anything**

with me. As for the one that is for you, it is your deeds, for which I shall recompense you when you need them most. As for the one that is between Me and you, it is prayer from you and acceptance from Me. As for the one that is between you and My creatures, treat people like you want them to treat you."""

The classification that this if for Allah and that is for the servant is regarding the love and contentment initially. The servant loves and wants what he sees fit for himself, and Allah (the Exalted) loves and approves the intended purpose in what pleases Him, and loves and approves the means subsequently. Otherwise, every commanded deed benefits the servant, and every commanded deed is loved by Allah and pleases Him. Therefore, whoever thinks that reliance is a public rank thinks that reliance is only good for the pursuit of worldly matters, which is wrong, as reliance in the religious affairs is greater.

Also, reliance is among the religious matters without which no compulsory or optional good deed can be complete. The person who is disinterested in it is disinterested in what Allah loves and commands and what pleases Him.

Lawful ascetism is disinterest in what does not benefit the person in the Hereafter, which refer to the excess of permitted things that are not used to help the person obey Allah.

Similarly, **lawful devoutness** is giving up what may harm the person in the Hereafter, i.e., leaving the forbidden deeds as well as the doubtful deeds as long as leaving them does not lead to leaving what is more certain, like the compulsory deeds. As for what benefits the person in the Hereafter or help him do what would be beneficial therein, disinterest in that is not religious. Rather the person who does that falls under Allah's saying: "*{O you who have believed, do not prohibit the good things which Allah has made lawful to you and do not transgress. Indeed, Allah does not like transgressors.}*" [5:87].

Moreover, preoccupation with the excess of permitted things is the opposite of the lawful asceticism. If it preoccupies the person from doing a compulsory deed or leads him to do a forbidden deed then he is a disobedient person. Otherwise, he drops from the rank of the Close Ones to the rank of the Moderate.

In addition, **reliance** is loved, approved and ever-commanded by Allah, and whatever is loved, approved and ever-commanded by Allah cannot be the deed of the moderate rather than the close ones. So, these are three answers for their claim: *"The relying person seeks …"*

Fate and Predestination

As for their claim that matters were already decided, this is similar to what some have said about supplication that there is no need for it, because if what you ask for was predetermined, the supplication is not needed, and if it was not predetermined, the supplication would not avail. This view is among the most corrupt views from the perspective of the Sharia and the sound reason.

Similarly, the claim that reliance and supplication do not bring benefit or prevent harm, but they are purely forms of worshipping, and that the essence of reliance is like the essence of an utter delegation. This view, even if some scholars uphold it, is also wrong.

The same applies for the view that supplication is purely a form of worshipping.

These views and the like stem from the same origin: It is that they thought that since matters are predetermined, this prevents them from depending on – also – predetermined causes from the servant. They did not know that Allah (the Exalted) predetermines and decrees matters with the causes on which He made them contingent such as the deeds of the servants and other causes. That's why going along with their view necessitates suspending deeds entirely.

The Prophet (PBUH) was asked about this "origin" several times and he answered.

It is stated in the Sahih book that Umran ibn Husain said: The Messenger (PBUH) was asked: *"O Allah's Messenger! Has there been drawn a distinction between the people of Paradise and the denizens of Hellfire?"* He said: *"**Yes.**"* He was asked: *"[If it is so], then what is the point of doing good deeds?"* Thereupon he said: *"**Everyone is facilitated in what has been created for him.**"*

It is also stated in the Sahih books that Ali ibn abu Talib said: We were accompanying a funeral procession with the Messenger (PBUH) and he sat with a small stick in his hand, so he started scraping the ground with it. He then said: *"**There is** *not a created soul, but has place either in Paradise or in Hell assigned for him and it is also determined for him whether he will be among the blessed or wretched.*" A man said: "*O Allah's Prophet (PBUH)! Should we not depend on what has been written for us and leave the deeds as whoever amongst us is blessed will do the deeds of a blessed person and whoever amongst us will be wretched, will do the deeds of a wretched person?*" The Prophet said: "**Work, for everyone is facilitated in what has been created for him. The good deeds are made easy for the blessed, and bad deeds are made easy for the wretched.**" Then he recited the Verses:"*{As for he who gives and fears Allah And believes in the best [reward], We will ease him toward ease. But as for he who withholds and considers himself free of need And denies the best [reward], We will ease him toward difficulty.}*" [92:5-10]. It was stated by the hadith scholars in the Sahih, Sunan and Musnad books.

Al-Tirmidhi narrated that the Prophet (PBUH) was asked: "'*Do you think that the medicines with which we treat ourselves, the Ruqyah by which we seek healing, and the means of protection that we seek, change the decree of Allah at all?*" He said: "**They are part of the decree of Allah.**"

This concept was narrated from the Prophet (PBUH) in multiple hadiths.

He (PBUH) clarified that the prior knowledge and writing of the blessed and the wretched does not contradict that the blessedness of the former is due to the good deeds, and the wretchedness of the latter is due to the evil deeds. He (the Exalted) knows the matters as they are, and He writes them as such. He knows that the blessed is blessed with the good deeds, and that the wretched is wretched with the evil deeds. Therefore, the blessed is guided to the good deeds that lead to blessedness, and the wretched is guided to the evil deeds that lead to wretchedness. Each of them is facilitated in what was created for him, which is what he will eventually reach of Allah's general universal will that He (the Exalted) mentioned in His Book in His saying: "*{... but they will not cease to differ, Except whom your Lord has given mercy, and for that He created them ...}*" [11:118-119].

The Classification of the Words, the Commands, the Will, the Permission, the Writing, the Decreeing, the Judgment and the Prohibition into Universal and Religious

As for that for which they were created, namely the love and satisfaction of Allah, which is His religious will, according to which they were commanded, this is mentioned in His saying: "*{And I did not create the jinn and mankind except to worship Me.}*" [51:56].

Allah (the Exalted) has distinguished in His book, for each of "the words", "the command", "the will", "the permission, "the book", "the decreeing", "the judgment", "the prohibition" and so on, between what is religious–i.e., conforms with the pleasure, satisfaction and legal command of Allah, and what is universal–i.e., conforms with His universal will.

An example for this is that He said concerning "the religious command": "*{Indeed, Allah orders justice and good conduct and giving [help] to relatives …}*" [16:90], "*{Indeed, Allah commands you to render trusts to whom they are due …}*" [4:58], and so on, and He said concerning "the universal command": "*{His command is only when He intends a thing that He says to it, "Be," and it is.}*" [36:82].

Similarly, His saying: "*{And when We intend to destroy a city, We command its affluent but they defiantly disobey therein; so the word [i.e., deserved decree] comes into effect upon it …}*" [17:16], according to one interpretation of this verse.

He also said about "the religious will": "*{… Allah intends for you ease and does not intend for you hardship …}*" [2:185], "*{Allah wants to make clear to you [the lawful from the unlawful] and guide you to the [good] practices of those before you and to accept your repentance. And Allah is Knowing and Wise.}*" [4:26], "*{… Allah does not intend to make difficulty for you, but He intends to purify you …}*" [5:6].

And he said regarding "the universal will": "*{… And if Allah had willed, they would not have fought each other, but Allah does what He intends.}*" [2:253], and said: "*{So whoever Allah wants to guide - He expands his breast to [contain] Islām; and whoever He wants to send astray - He makes his breast tight and constricted as though he were climbing into the sky …}*" [6:125].

Noah (PBUH) said: "*{And my advice will not benefit you - although I wished to advise you - if Allah should intend to put you in error …}*" [11:34]

He (the Exalted) also said: "*{His command is only when He intends a thing that He says to it, "Be," and it is.}*" [36:82].

Allah (the Exalted) said regarding "the religious permission": "*{Whatever you have cut down of [their] palm trees or left standing on their trunks - it was by permission of Allah and so He would disgrace the defiantly disobedient.}*" [59:5]

And regarding "the universal permission": "*{… But they do not harm anyone through it except by permission of Allah …}*" [2:102].

Allah (the Exalted) said concerning "the religious decreeing": "*{And your Lord has decreed that you worship not except Him …}*" [17:23], decreed here meaning: commanded.

He (the Exalted) also said concerning "the universal decreeing": "*{And He decreed [i.e., completed] them as seven heavens within two days …}*" [41:12].

Allah (the Exalted) said regarding "the religious judgment": "*{… Lawful for you are the animals of grazing livestock except for* *that which is recited to you [in this Qur'ān] - hunting not being permitted while you are in the state of iḥrām. Indeed, Allah ordains what He intends.}* " [5:1], and said: "*{... That is the judgement of Allah; He judges between you ...}*" [60:10].

He (the Exalted) said concerning "the universal judgment", conveying from the son of Jacob (PBUH): "*{... So I will never leave [this] land until my father permits me or Allah decides for me, and He is the best of judges.}*" [12:80], and He (the Exalted) also said: "*{[The Prophet (PBUH)] has said: "My Lord, judge [between us] in truth. And our Lord is the Most Merciful, the one whose help is sought against that which you describe."}*" [21:112].

Allah (the Exalted) said regarding "the religious prohibition": "*{Prohibited to you are dead animals, blood, the flesh of swine ...}*" [5:3], "{

Prohibited to you [for marriage] are your mothers, your daughters ...}" [4:23], until the end of the verse. On the other hand, He said concerning "the universal prohibition": "*{[Allah] said, "Then indeed, it is forbidden to them for forty years [in which] they will wander throughout the land ...}*" [5:26]. He (the Exalted) also said: "*{And those within whose wealth is a known right - For the petitioner and the deprived[4].}*" [70:24-25].

Allah (the Exalted) said regarding "the religious words": "*{And [mention, O Muhammad], when Abraham was tried by his Lord with words [i.e., commands] and he fulfilled them ...}*" [2:124]. He (the Exalted) said regarding "the universal words": "*{... And the good word [i.e., decree] of your Lord was fulfilled for the Children of Israel because of what they had patiently endured ...}*" [7:137].

Another example for this is the saying of the Prophet (PBUH) which was narrated from him in different versions in the Sahih, Sunan and Musnad books, that he (PBUH) used to say in his deprecation: "*I seek refuge in the Perfect Words of Allah, which neither the upright nor the corrupt may overcome.*" It is well-known that this refers to the universal words in which none can escape His will and creation, as for the religious words, the corrupt have gone against them by disobeying Him.

---

[4] The Arabic words for "prohibit" and "deprive" are derived from the same origin.

The point here is that he (PBUH) clarified that people are facilitated towards the outcomes for which they were created, such as blessedness and wretchedness, and it is the same for all creatures. He (the Exalted) creates the infant of humans and all animals in the wombs through the sexual intercourse that He decrees between the parents, and the combination of the sperm and the ovule in the womb. So, if a man said: *"I will rely on Allah and refrain from having intercourse with my wife, and if a child is decreed for me, he/she will come to existence. Otherwise, he/she will not come to existence and there is no need for intercourse,"* then he is a fool. This is different than if he has intercourse and decides to practice coitus interruptus, because this does not prevent impregnation if Allah wills, for the semen may be discharged before he can do that.

An example for this is what was narrated in the Sahih books by Abu Saied al-Khudri, who said: We accompanied the Messenger (PBUH) during the battle with Bani al-Mustaliq, and we captured some females and intended to have sexual relation with them without impregnating them. So we asked the Prophet (PBUH) about coitus interruptus. The Prophet (PBUH) said: **"It is better for you not to do it, for Allah has written whom He is going to create till the Day of Resurrection."** It is also narrated in Sahih Muslim by Jabir that a man came to the Prophet (PBUH) and said: *"I have a slave-girl who is our servant and she carries water for us and I have intercourse with her, but I do not want her to conceive."* He (PBUH) said: **"Practice coitus interruptus, if you so like, but what is decreed for her will come to her."**

This is despite that fact that Allah (the Exalted) is capable of doing what He has already done, i.e., to create a human being without parents—as He did with Adam (PBUH), to create a human being from a father alone—as He did with Eve, and to create a human being from a mother alone—as He created Jesus the son of Mary (PBUH). However, He created those with other, unusual means.

This concept, although it is denied by the infidels who undermine divine legislations, many glorified sheikhs have stumbled onto its subtleties. Some of them go too far with predestination without observing what they were commanded and prohibited to do, and they consider that to fall under reliance, delegation and going along with the fatalistic truth. They think that the statement that says: "A servant must be with Allah like a corpse at the hands of the washer," entails disregarding the command and the prohibition until the person neglects what he is commanded to do and commits what he is forbidden to do, and until the light and the standard, with which he distinguishes what Allah commands, loves and approves from what Allah forbids, hates and despises, is weakened, leading him to make equal what Allah made unequal.

As Allah (the Exalted) said: "*{Or do those who commit evils think We will make them like those who have believed and done righteous deeds - [make them] equal in their life and their death? Evil is that which they judge [i.e., assume].}*" [45:21], "*{Then will We treat the Muslims like the criminals? What is [the matter] with you? How do you judge?}*" [68:35-36], "*{Or should We treat those who believe and do righteous deeds like corrupters in the land? Or should We treat those who fear Allah like the wicked?}*" [38:28], "*{... Say: "Are those who know equal to those who do not know?" ...}*" [39:9], "*{Not equal are the blind and the seeing, nor are the darknesses and the light, nor are the shade and the heat, and not equal are the living and the dead. Indeed, Allah causes to hear whom He wills, but you cannot make hear those in the graves.}*" [35:19-22], and so on.

The fanatics among them end up making no distinction between the legal, religious, criterial, divine and prophetic command which is indicated by the Book and the Sunnah, and between the incidents that occur at the hands of the infidels and the wicked. They witness the commonality that everything happens with the Allah's decree, predestination, Lordship and general will, and that everything is within His dominion, but they do not witness the distinction that Allah made between His allies and His enemies, the righteous and the wicked, the believers and the infidels, the people of obedience who obeyed His religious command, and the people of disobedience who disobeyed this religious command. They cite as evidence some abridged statements that were conveyed from some scholars, or some errors of some of them.

This is a "great principle" and one of the matters that should be most observed by the people on the way to Allah who walk the path of will: the will of those who seek His countenance, as the negligence of which has led groups of them to engage in disbelief, defiance and disobedience to the extent that only Allah knows, so much so that they became helpers in injustice and aggression to the people of injustice and haughtiness whom Allah empowered on earth. For example, those who turn with their hearts towards helping the people of injustice and haughtiness to whom they are inclined, thinking that if they had states with which they made an impact thereon, they would be allies of Allah – **for the impact of hearts is greater than that of the bodies**. However, if the hearts are sound, their impact is sound, and if they are corrupt, their impact is corrupt. The impact of states is approved by Allah sometimes and disapproved other times.

The jurists spoke about the obligation of retaliation against whoever kills another in secret, for retaliation is a must in this case – they cite their hearts and inward natures as evidence for the universal matter, and they consider the mere breaking of the ordinary, through an unveiling made to him or an impact conforming to his will as a miracle from Allah for him. They are not aware that it is in fact a seduction, and that a miracle is the consequence of uprightness, and that Allah does not honor His servant with a miracle greater than making him conform to what He loves and approves, namely the obedience of Allah, the obedience of His Messenger, the alliance with His allies and the resentment of His enemies.

Those are the allies of Allah, about whom Allah said: "**{Unquestionably, [for] the allies of Allah there will be no fear concerning them, nor will they grieve.}**" [10:62].

If they conform to what Allah imposed upon them, then they are among **the moderate**, and if they conform to what He imposed and loved, then they are among **the close ones**, noting that every obligatory deed is loved, while not every loved deed is obligatory.

CHAPTER 9

The Supernatural

As for the ease, supernatural or otherwise, or hardship with which Allah tries His servant, it is neither for the honor nor the degradation of the servant by his Lord. Rather, some people may be blessed by that if they obey Allah therein, and some may be wretched by it if they disobey Him therein.

Allah (the Exalted) said: "*{And as for man, when his Lord tries him and [thus] is generous to him and favors him, he says: "My Lord has honored me." But when He tries him and restricts his provision, he says: "My Lord has humiliated me." No! ...}*" [89:15-17]. This is why people are classified into three categories in these matters:

- People who rise in ranks through the supernatural by using it in obedience of Allah.

- People who are exposed to the wrath of Allah through it if they use it in disobedience of Allah, such as Balaam and others.
- People who are neutral in that regard.

The first group are the true believers who follow their Prophet, the master of all the children of Adam, whose miracles were for an argument to establish the religion of Allah or to help him obey Allah. Due to the frequent confusion regarding this principle, the Prophet (PBUH) forbade going too far with predestination without keenness on doing the commands that benefit the servant. Muslim stated in his Sahih what Abu Hurairah narrated, that the Messenger (PBUH) said: "**A believer who is strong is better and dearer to Allah than the weak believer, but there is goodness in both of them. Be keen on what benefits you and seek help from Allah, and do not give up. If anything afflicts you do not say: "If I had done such and such things, such and such would have happened." But say: "Allah decrees and what He wills He does," for (the utterance) 'If I had' provides an opening for the deeds of the devil.**"

It is stated in Sunan Abu Dawud that two men disputed each other to the Prophet (PBUH) and he ruled against one of them, so that person, against whom he ruled, said: "*Sufficient for us is*

Allah, and [He is] the best Disposer of affairs." The Prophet (PBUH) said: "**Allah blames for falling short, but apply intelligence, and when the matter gets the better of you, say: Sufficient for us is Allah, and [He is] the best Disposer of affairs.**" Thereupon, the Prophet (PBUH) commanded the believer to be keen on what benefits him and seek the help of Allah, which matches Allah's (the Exalted) saying: "*{It is You we worship and You we ask for help.}*" [1:5], and His saying: "*{... so worship Him and rely upon Him ...}*" [11:123]. Keenness on what benefits the servant refers to obeying and worshipping Allah, for what benefits the servant is Allah's obedience, and nothing else is more beneficial to him. Everything that helps one worship Allah is considered as a form of worshipping, even if it were a permitted thing [i.e. neither commanded nor prohibited].

The Prophet (PBUH) said in the authentic hadith narrated by Saad: "**You will be rewarded for whatever you spend for Allah's sake even if it were a morsel which you put in your wife's mouth.**"

The Prophet (PBUH) informed us that Allah blames for falling short, which is opposite to intelligence, and which means neglecting what one was commanded to do, for this contradicts the ability that is coupled with the verb, although it does not contradict the aforementioned ability, which is the basis for the command and the prohibition.

The ability that necessitates that verb is coupled with it and is not fit except for its subject, as Allah (the Exalted) mention in His saying: "*{... They were not able to hear ...}*" [11:20], and His saying: "*{... and they were not able to hear.}*" [18:101]. As for the ability upon which the command and the prohibition are based, it may or may not be coupled with the verb, as in His saying: "*{... And [due] to Allah from the people is a pilgrimage to the House - for whoever is able to find thereto a way ...}*" [3:97], and the Prophet's (PBUH) saying to Imran ibn Hussain: "**Pray standing and if you are unable, pray sitting and if you cannot, pray lying on your side.**"

In this matter, people are divided into four groups:

(1) A group of people who consider the aspects of the command, the prohibition, the worshipping and the obedience, bearing witness to the divinity of the Almighty Lord whom they were commanded to worship, but who do not consider the aspects of predestination, fate, reliance and seeking help [from Allah]. This is the state of many students of jurisprudence and worshipper-

wannabes. Despite their good intentions and their honoring of the sacred ordinances [and rites] of Allah, they are predominated by weakness, helplessness and disappointment, because seeking the help of Allah, reliance upon Him, seeking refuge in Him and supplicating to Him are what strengthen the servant and facilitate matters for him.

This is why some early scholar said: *"Whoever wishes to be the strongest of people should rely upon Allah."*

His (PBUH) Description in the Torah

It is narrated in Sahih al-Bukhari and Sahih Muslim from Abdullah ibn Amr that the Messenger (PBUH) is described in the Torah as follows: ***"Verily We have sent you (O Muhammad) as a witness, as a bringer of glad tidings and as a warner, and as a protector for the illiterates (i.e., the Arabs.) You are my servant and My messenger, and I have named you Al-Mutawakkil (one who relies upon Allah). You are neither hard-hearted nor of fierce character, nor one who shouts in the markets. You do not return evil for evil, but excuse and forgive. Allah will not take you unto Him till He guides through you a crocked (curved) nation on the right path, so I will open,*** *through you, blind eyes, deaf ears and hardened hearts by causing them to say: "There is no deity except Allah."*"

This is why it was narrated that the Bearers of the Throne could only bear the Throne by saying: *"There is no power or might except with Allah,"* and it was stated in the Sahih books that the Prophet (PBUH) said: *"It is one of the treasures of Paradise."* Allah (the Exalted) said: *"{... And whoever relies upon Allah - then He is sufficient for him ...}"* [65:3], His saying: *"{Those to whom people [i.e., hypocrites] said: "Indeed, the people have gathered against you, so fear them." But it [merely] increased them in faith, and they said: "Sufficient for us is Allah, and [He is] the best Disposer of affairs."}"* until His saying: *"{... So fear them not, but fear Me, if you are [indeed] believers.}"* [3:173-175]. It is also stated in Sahih al-Bukhari that Ibn Abbas (may Allah be pleased with him) said, in interpretation of the verse: *"{and they said: "Sufficient for us is Allah, and [He is] the best Disposer of affairs."}"*: *"Ibrahim (Abraham) said it when he was thrown into the fire, so did Muhammad (PBUH) when he was told: "Indeed, the people have gathered against you ..."*"

(2) A second group of people who bear witness to the lordship of Allah the Truth and their neediness of Him and they seek His help, but according to their

inclinations and tastes, without considering the truth of His command, prohibition, pleasure, dissatisfaction and love. This is the state of many ascetics and hermits. This is why they work according the states which they manage in the world, without seeking what the Lord approves and loves. They often err and think that disobeying Him is what pleases Him, so they go back to suspending commands and prohibitions and call that 'a truth', and they think that they must go along with this fatalistic truth without observing the religious imperatival truth, which contains the Lord's satisfaction, love, command and prohibition both apparently and inapparently.

These are frequently deprived of their states and may revert to a form of disobedience and defiance. Rather, many of them renounce Islam, because the best outcome is for those of righteousness, and whoever does not respect Allah's command and prohibition is not righteous. They do some of what the polytheists do, such as regarding a novelty as a religious legislation, and citing predestination as evidence against the command [of Allah]. When Allah (the Exalted) mentioned criticism of the polytheists in Surah al-An'am and Surah al-A'raf[5], He mentioned what they innovated in the religion and made into a law, as He (the Exalted) said: "*{And when they commit an immorality, they say: "We found our fathers doing it, and Allah has ordered us to do it." Say: "Indeed, Allah does not order immorality ...}*" [7:28]. He also vilified them for forbidding what Allah did not forbid, and ordaining what Allah did not ordain, and He mentioned their use of predestination as an argument, in His saying: "*{Those who associated [others] with Allah will say: "If Allah had willed, we would not have associated [anything] and neither would our fathers, nor would we have prohibited anything." ...}*" [6:148]. Similar verses are mentioned in Surah al-Nahl, Ya-sin and al-Zukhruf[6].

(3) As for **the third group**: it is those who have turned away from worshipping Allah and seeking his help, which is the most wretched group.

(4) **The fourth group** is the praiseworthy group, which refers to those who achieved His saying: "*{It is You we worship and You we ask for help.}*" [1:5], and His saying: "*{... so worship Him and rely upon Him ...}*" [11:123]. Thus, they sought His help in obeying Him, testified that He is their deity, none other than whom

---

[5] The 6th and 7th chapters of the Holy Qur'an, respectively.
[6] The 16th, 36th and 43rd chapters of the Holy Qur'an, respectively.

may be worshipped, by obeying Him and obeying His messenger, and they testified that He is their Lord, and that "*{besides Him there will be no protector and no intercessor for them …}*" [6:51] and that "*{Whatever Allah grants to people of mercy - none can withhold it; and whatever He withholds - none can release it thereafter …}*" [35:2], "*{And if Allah should touch you with adversity, there is no remover of it except Him; and if He intends for you good, then there is no repeller of His bounty …}*" [10:107], "*{… Say: "Then have you considered what you invoke besides Allah? If Allah intended me harm, are they removers of His harm; or if He intended me mercy, are they withholders of His mercy?" …}*" [39:38].

This is why a group of scholars said that turning towards means is association in Tawhid (belief in Allah's oneness), not considering means to be means is a deficiency in intellect, and turning away from means completely is defamation of the Sharia. However, the commanded reliance is what combines the requirements of Tawhid, intellect and Sharia.

It is now shown that whoever thought that reliance is a rank of the general public is heavily mistaken, even if he was a renowned scholar – such as the author of "Ilal al-Maqamaat

(The Faults of the Ranks)" who is among the most glorified scholars, and the author of "Mahasin al-Majalis (The Virtues of Councils)" learned that from him – and the weakness of such argument was shown because it assumes that the purpose of reliance is the share of the general public. Whoever assumes that is no different than whoever assumes the same concerning the other commanded deeds, such as whoever preoccupied himself with reliance from the means that he should seek to acquire, which in itself is ordained worshipping and obedience. The error of the former in neglecting the ordained means that are included in His saying: "*{... so worship Him and rely upon Him ...}*" is equal to the error of the latter in neglecting the ordained reliance that is included in His saying: "*{... so worship Him and rely upon Him ...}*" [11:123].

Instead, we say: The person whose reliance upon Allah and supplication to Him is for the realization of permitted [worldly] matters, then he is of the general public, and if it is for the realization of recommended and obligatory [religious] matters, then he is of the select few. Additionally, whoever supplicates to Allah and relies upon Him for the realization of forbidden things, then he is of those who wrong themselves, and whoever turns away from reliance is disobedient to Allah and His

Messenger, or rather deviant from the truth of faith, so how can this rank be exclusive for the select few? Allah (the Exalted) said: "*{And Moses said: "O my people, if you have believed in Allah, then rely upon Him, if you should be Muslims [i.e., submitting to Him]."}*" [10:84]. He also said: "*{If Allah should aid you, no one can overcome you; but if He should forsake you, who is there that can aid you after Him? And upon Allah let the believers rely.}*" [3:160]. He also said: "*{Say: "Then have you considered what you invoke besides Allah? If Allah intended me harm, are they removers of His harm…}*" until His saying: "*{Say: "Sufficient for me is Allah; upon Him [alone] rely the [wise] reliers."}*" [39:38].

Allah mentioned this phrase: "**Sufficient for me is Allah**" in bringing benefit one time and in pushing harm away another time. **The former** is in His saying: "*{If only they had been satisfied with what Allah and His Messenger gave them and said: "Sufficient for us is Allah; Allah will give us of His bounty, and [so will] His Messenger …}*" until the end of the verse [9:59]. **The latter** is in His saying: "*{Those to whom people [i.e., hypocrites] said, "Indeed, the people have gathered against you, so fear them." But it [merely] increased them in faith, and they said, "Sufficient for us is Allah, and [He is] the best*

Disposer of affairs."}" [3:173], and His saying: "*{But if they intend to deceive you - then sufficient for you is Allah. It is He who supported you with His help and with the believers}*" [8:62]. The verse: "*{If only they had been satisfied with what Allah and His Messenger gave them and said: "Sufficient for us is Allah; Allah will give us of His bounty, and [so will] His Messenger ...}*" [9:59] includes the command for contentment and reliance.

Contentment and reliance surround the predestined matter, reliance precedes it, and contentment follows it. This is why the Prophet (PBUH) used to say in prayer: "***O Allah, by Your Knowledge of the unseen and by Your Power over creation, let me live if You know that life is good for me, and let me die if You know that death is good for me. O Allah, I ask You to grant me fear of You in private and in public. I ask you for the word of truth in times of contentment and anger. I ask You for moderation in wealth and in poverty. I ask you for blessings never ceasing and the comfort of my eye (i.e., pleasure) that never ends. I ask You for contentment after Your decree, and I ask You for a life of coolness after death. I ask You for the delight of gazing upon Your Face, and the joy of meeting You, without any harm and misleading trials befalling me. O Allah,***

dress us with the beauty of Faith and make us guides who are upon (correct) guidance." Stated by Ahmad and al-Nasa'y as narrated by Ammar ibn Yasir.

Refraining from Exposing Oneself to Trial

What precedes the predestined matter is a resolve for contentment, and not contentment itself.

This is why a group of Sheikhs used to make a resolve for contentment before misfortune happens, and when it did, their resolves were broken, similar to what happens with forbearance and whatnot. Allah (the Exalted) said: "***{And you had certainly wished for death [i.e., martyrdom] before you encountered it, and you have [now] seen it [before you] while you were looking on.}***" [3:143]. He (the Exalted) also said: "***{O you who have believed, why do you say what you do not do? Greatly hateful in the sight of Allah is that you say what you do not do. Indeed, Allah loves those who fight in His cause in a row as though they are a [single] structure joined firmly.}***" [61:2-4]. These verses were revealed when they said: "*If we knew which deed is dearest to Allah, we would do it.*" Thereupon, Allah revealed the verse of Jihad, but many people disliked it.

This is why it is disapproved for the person to expose himself to trial, by imposing upon himself what Allah did not impose upon him with covenants, vows and so on, or to request a position of authority or enter a place where a plague has spread.

It is stated in the Sahih books through multiple chains of narration that the Prophet (PBUH) discouraged vowing and said: "*It does not [necessarily] bring good, but it is means to extract wealth from the miserly.*" It is also stated in the Sahih books that he (PBUH) said to Abdurrahman ibn Samurah: "*Do not ask for a position of authority, for if you are granted this position as a result of your asking for it, you will be left alone (without God's help to discharge the responsibilities attendant thereon), and it you are granted it without making any request for it, you will be helped (by God in the discharge of your duties), and whenever you take an oath to do something and later you find that something else is better than the first, then do the better one and make expiation for your oath.*" It is also stated in the Sahih books that he said about the plague: "*If you hear that it (plague) has broken out in a land, do not go to it; but if it breaks out in a land where you are present, do not go out escaping from it.*" It is also stated in the Sahih books that he (PBUH) said: "*O people! Do not long for encountering*

the enemy and supplicate to Allah to grant you security. But when you face the enemy, show patience and steadfastness; and keep it in mind that Jannah lies under the shade of the swords." There are many such examples which entail that the person should not do what imposes [or forbids] things upon himself lest he cannot fulfil that, like many who make covenants with Allah, and most of them are tried with the breaking of their covenants.

Forbearance and its Provisions

These hadiths also entail that when a man is tried, he must endure, stand firm and not recoil in order to be among the people who are certain in belief and who fulfil their duties. Forbearance is a must in all that. This is why forbearance is compulsory, as per the consensus of Muslims, for carrying out obligatory deeds and refraining from forbidden deeds. This also includes endurance of afflictions, and resisting the soul's temptations in what Allah forbade.

Allah mentioned patience in over ninety instances in His Book, and he coupled it with the prayer in His saying: "*{And seek help through patience and prayer; and indeed, it is difficult except for the humbly submissive [to Allah]}*" [2:45], His saying: "*{... seek help through patience and prayer. Indeed, Allah is with the patient.}*" [2:153], His saying: "*{And establish prayer at the two ends of the day and at the approach of the night ...}*" until His saying: "*{And be patient, for indeed, Allah does not allow to be lost the reward of those who do good.}*" [11:114-115], His saying: "*{So be patient over what they say and exalt [Allah] with praise of your Lord before the rising of the sun and before its setting ...}*" [20:130], His saying: "*{So be patient, [O Muhammad]. Indeed, the promise of Allah is truth. And ask forgiveness for your sin ...}*" until the end of the verse [40:55].

He made "religious leadership" inherited through patience and certainty, in His saying: "*{And We made from among them leaders guiding by Our command when they were patient and [when] they were certain of Our signs.}*" [32:24]. The entire religion consists of knowing the truth and applying it, and applying it requires certainty and patience. Even the pursuit of its knowledge requires patience, as Mu'adh ibn Jabal (may Allah be pleased with him) said: *"You should pursue knowledge,* *because pursuing it for the sake of Allah is a form of worshipping, knowing it leads to fear [of Allah], seeking it is a form of Jihad, teaching it to whoever doesn't know it is charity and studying it is a form of exaltation. With it, Allah is known and worshipped, and with it, Allah is glorified and declared as One. Through knowledge, Allah raises some people and makes them leaders and Imams for the people, to use as beacons of guidance and to seek their opinion."*

Therefore, he regarded the pursuit of knowledge as Jihad, and Jihad requires forbearance. This is why Allah (the Exalted) said: "**{By time, Indeed, mankind is in loss, Except for those who have believed and done righteous deeds and advised each other to truth and advised each other to patience.}**" [103:1-3]. He also said: "**{And remember Our servants, Abraham, Isaac and Jacob - those of strength and [religious] vision.}**" [38:45].

The beneficial knowledge is the origin of guidance, and knowledge of the truth is the right course. The opposite of the former is misguidance, and the opposite of the latter is error. Misguidance is acting without knowledge, and error is following desires. He (the Exalted) said: "**{Your companion [i.e., Muhammad] has not strayed, nor has he erred}**" [53:2]. Guidance is not attained except with knowledge, and the right course is not attained except with forbearance. This is why Ali said: *"Verily, forbearance to faith is like the head to the body – if the head is severed, the body crumbles,"* then he raised his voice and said: *"Verily, there is no faith for him who has no forbearance."*

Contentment and its Provisions

As for **contentment**, the companions of Imam Ahmad of scholars and sheikhs debated about the contentment with fate: is it obligatory or desirable? They were divided into two views: **the first** is that it is of the deeds of the moderate, and **the second** is that it is of the deeds of the close ones. Umar ibn Abdulaziz said: *"Contentment is rare, but forbearance is the believer's pickaxe."* It is narrated that the Prophet (PBUH) said to Ibn Abbas: **"If you can practice, for the sake of Allah, contentment with certainty, do so. Otherwise, endurance of what you hate holds a lot of good."**

This is why nothing is mentioned in the Qur'an except praise for the content, and not the obligation of such. This is concerning contentment with what Allah does to His servant of trials, such as illness, poverty and shaking, as Allah (the Exalted) said: "*{... and [those who] are patient in poverty and hardship and during battle ...}*" [2:177]. He (the Exalted) also said: "*{Or do you think that you will enter Paradise while such [trial] has not yet come to you as came to those who passed on before you? They were touched by poverty and hardship and were shaken ...}*" [2:214]. Poverty is a trial in wealth, hardship is in the body and the shaking is in the heart.

As for **contentment with what Allah commanded** it is compulsory, and it is faith, as the Prophet (PBUH) said in the authentic hadith: "*He has found the taste of faith–he who is content with Allah as his Lord, with Islam as his religion and with Muhammad (PBUH) as his Prophet.*"

It is also among the consequences of love, as we will mention later, God willing. Allah (the Exalted) said: "*{But no, by your Lord, they will not [truly] believe until they make you, [O Muhammad], judge concerning that over which they dispute among themselves and then find within themselves no discomfort from what you have judged and submit in [full, willing] submission.}*" [4:65]. He (the Exalted) also said: "*{If only they had been satisfied with what Allah and His*

Messenger gave them and said: "Sufficient for us is Allah ...}" until the end of the verse [9:59].

He (the Exalted) also said: "*{That is because they followed what angered Allah and disliked [what earns] His pleasure, so He rendered worthless their deeds.}*" [47:28]. He also said: "*{And what prevents their expenditures from being accepted from them but that they have disbelieved in Allah and in His Messenger and that they come not to prayer except while they are lazy and that they do not spend except while they are unwilling.}*" [9:54].

Among the examples for the first type is what Ahmad, al-Tirmidhi and others stated as narrated by Saad that the Prophet (PBUH) said: "*Among [the signs of] the person's blessedness, is his contentment with what Allah decreed for him, and among [the signs of] the person's misery is his avoiding to request counsel from Allah, and his dissatisfaction with what Allah decreed for him.*"

As for **contentment with forbidden deeds** such as disbelief, defiance and disobedience, most scholars agree that it is not lawful for one to be content with them or to love them.

Allah (the Exalted) does not approve of them or love them, even if He decreed and predestined them, as He (the Exalted) said: "*{... And Allah does not like corruption.}*" [2:205]. He (the Exalted) also said: "*{... And He does not approve for His servants disbelief ...}*" [29:7]. He also said: "*{... and He is with them [in His knowledge] when they spend the night in such as He does not accept of speech ...}*" [4:108]. Rather, He is angered by them, as He (the Exalted) said: "*{That is because they followed what angered Allah and disliked [what earns] His pleasure, so He rendered worthless their deeds.}*" [47:28].

A group of scholars said that one should be content with them from the aspect of being attributed to Allah in creation, and be discontent from the aspect of being attributed to the servant in action. This view does not contradict the previous one, as both of them stem from the same principle. He (the Exalted) predestined and created the things for a wisdom.

In consideration of that wisdom, these acts are loved and accepted, although they may be despised and disapproved in themselves. The single matter may have two attributes, one of them is loved by the person while the other is hated, as in the authentic hadith: "*... and I do not hesitate to do anything as I* *hesitate to take the soul of the believer, for he hates death, and I hate to disappoint him, but there is no escaping it."*

As for whoever argues for contentment with the predestination, which is the attribute and action of Allah, and not with the predestined matter, which is the object of such action, he has gone out of topic. The subject is not contentment with the attributes and actions of the Lord (the Exalted), but it is about contentment with the objects of His actions. We have clarified what is related to this point elsewhere.

Of Perfect Contentment: Praise

The perfectness of **contentment**, which is one of the deeds of the hearts, is praise. Some scholars even interpreted gratitude as contentment. This is why the praise of Allah was mentioned in the Book and the Sunnah, which includes contentment with His predestination. The hadith says: *"The first people to be called to Paradise are the praisers who praise Allah in secret and in openness."* It is narrated that when something happened that pleased the Prophet (PBUH), the Prophet (PBUH) used to say: *"Praise is to Allah by whose blessings all good things are perfected."* And if something happened that displeased him, he used to say: *"**Praise is to Allah in all circumstances.**"*

It is also stated in Musnad Ahmad, as narrated by Abu Moussa al-Ash'ary that the Prophet (PBUH) said: *"**If the servant's child dies, Allah says to His angels: "Did you take the soul of my servant's child?" They say: "Yes." He says: "Did you take the fruit of his heart?" They say: "Yes." He says: "What did my servant say?" They say: "He praised you and said: "To Allah we belong and to Him we shall return.""" He says: "Build a house for my servant in Paradise and call it: the House of Praise.""*

Our Prophet Muhammad (PBUH) is the holder of the Banner of Praise, and his Ummah are the praisers who praise Allah for the ease and the hardship. Praise in hardship is contingent on two scenes:

(First): The servant's knowledge that Allah is worthy of praise, as He perfected everything which He created, and He is the Knowing, the Wise, the Aware, the Merciful.

(Second): His knowledge that Allah's choice for the believing servant is better than his own choice for himself. It is narrated in Sahih Muslim and elsewhere that the Prophet (PBUH) said:

"By Him in whose hand my soul is, nothing is decreed for the believer except it is good for him, and this is only for the believer: if ease comes to him, he praises [Allah], so it is good for him, and if hardship befalls him, he endures, so it is good for him."

Therefore, the Prophet (PBUH) clarifies that every predestination decreed by Allah for the believer, who endures affliction and praises for ease, is good for him.

He (the Exalted) said: "***{Indeed in that are signs for everyone patient and grateful.}***" [31:31]

And he mentioned these two traits together in four instances of His Book.

As for whoever does not endure affliction and does not show gratitude for ease, the predestination is not necessarily good for him. Therefore, I respond to whoever uses this hadith as an argument concerning the sins that are predestined for the believer with two responses:

(First): This hadith discusses what happens to the servant, and not what the servant does, as in Allah's saying: "***{What comes to you of good is from Allah ...}***" referring to ease, "***{... but***

what comes to you of evil, [O man], is from yourself ...}" [4:79] referring to hardship, and as in Allah's saying: "*{... And We tested them with good [times] and bad that perhaps they would return [to obedience]}*" [7:168], i.e., with ease and hardship. Also as He (the Exalted) said: "*{... And We test you with evil and with good as trial ...}*" [21:35], and said: "*{If good touches you, it distresses them; but if harm strikes you, they rejoice at it ...}*" [3:120]. Therefore, good and bad in the verses can mean ease and hardship, or good and evil deeds.

(Second): This hadith refers to the forbearing and praising believer, **but sins reduce faith**. If the servant repents, Allah loves him, and his rank may increase with the repentance. **Some early scholar said:** "*David (PBUH) was better after repentance than he was before the sin.*" Whoever is predestined to repent is like what **Saied ibn Jubair** said: "*A person may do a good deed and enter Hellfire because of it, and he may do a baddeed and enter Paradise because of it. This is because when he does a good deed, it is there in front of him and he admires it, and when he does a bad deed, it is there in front of him, and he ask's Allah for forgiveness and repents therefrom.*" It is narrated in the Sahih that the Prophet (PBUH) said: "**Judgement is given according to one's final deeds.**"

Ibn Taymiyyah

The Marks of the Sincere Repentance

When the believer commits a sin, he can be relieved of its punishment through ten means:

(1) If he repents and Allah accepts his repentance, for he who repents from sin is like he who have no sin.
(2) If he asks forgiveness and is forgiven.
(3) If he does good deeds that erase the sin, for good deeds do away with misdeeds.
(4) If his believing brothers pray and ask forgiveness on his behalf, both in his life and after his death.
(5) If they confer some of the reward of their good deeds upon him.
(6) If Prophet Muhammad (PBUH) intercedes on his behalf.
(7) If Allah tries him in the worldly life with afflictions that expatiate for his sin.
(8) If Allah tries him in the barrier [grave] with the shock and expatiate his sin with that.
(9) If Allah tries him in the horrors of the Day of Judgment with what expatiates for his sin.

(10) If the Most Merciful of the merciful shows him mercy.

Whoever misses all ten of these should blame no one besides himself, as Allah (the Exalted) said, as narrated by His Messenger (PBUH): "*O My servants, it is but your deeds that I record for you and then recompense you for. So let him who finds good praise Allah, and let him who finds other than that blame no one but himself.*"

If the believer knew that the predestination is good for him if he is forbearing and grateful, or if he sought Allah's counsel and knew that it is a blessing for the servant to seek Allah's counsel and be content with what He decreed for him, he would be content with what is better for him.

In the authentic hadith narrated by Ali (may Allah be pleased with him): "*Allah decrees the matter, so whoever is content, Allah is content with him, and whoever is discontent, Allah is discontent with him.*"

This hadith includes contentment and seeking Allah's counsel. Contentment follows the predestined matter, while seeking Allah's counsel precedes it. This is more fitting than hardship and forbearance. This is why he mentioned contentment here and forbearance there.

And if the predestined matter is combined with forbearance is good for the person, so how about if it is combined with contentment? Thus, the hadith said: *"The aggrieved is one who is deprived of the reward."* in the story narrated by al-Shafi'y in his Musnad, that when the Prophet (PBUH) passed away, they heard a caller say: *"O people of the house of the Messenger (PBUH)! In Allah there is consolation for every calamity, compensation for every mortal, and recovery for every lost thing. So, trust in Allah and hope in Him, for the aggrieved is one who is deprived of the reward."* This is why the grief that is contradictory to contentment was never commanded. Although it has no benefit, it may cause harm. However, it is pardoned if it was not coupled with what Allah dislikes.

Nevertheless, weeping over the dead out of compassion is good and desirable, and it does not contradict contentment, unlike weeping for parting with the dead. This is how we understand the saying of the Prophet (PBUH) when he wept over a dead person: **"This is mercy which Allah has put in the heart of His servants, and Allah bestows His mercy only on those of His slaves who are merciful (to others)."** This is unlike whoever weeps for his own sake, and not out of compassion with the deceased. The state of al-Fudayl ibn Iyadh when his son died, he laughed and said: "*I saw that Allah has made a decree, so I wanted to be content with what Allah decreed,*" is better than the state of the people of impatience. However, compassion with the deceased along with contentment with the decree and praise for Allah (the Exalted), such as the state of the Prophet (PBUH), is more perfect. Allah (the Exalted) said: "**{and—above all—to be one of those who have faith and urge each other to perseverance and urge each other to compassion.}**" [90:17]. He (the Exalted) mentioned urging each other to perseverance and compassion.

People are divided into four categories: (1) some of them exhibit endurance with toughness, (2) some exhibit compassion with impatience, (3) some exhibit toughness and impatience, (4) and the praiseworthy believer is the one who endures what befalls him while showing compassion to the people.

Some of the authors in this topic thought that contentment with Allah is a consequence of love for Him. This only considers "the first aspect", which is contentment with Him because He Himself is worthy of that, regardless of the servant's share, unlike "the second aspect", which is contentment because the servant knows that the predestined matter is better for him. Moreover, love is related to Him, while contentment is related to His decreeing. However, it may be said, in agreement with what such author have said, that there are two types of love for Allah: love for Him Himself, and love for His beneficence. Similarly, there are two types of praise for Him: praise for what He Himself deserves, and praise for His beneficence to His servant. The two types of contentment are like the two types of love.

As for contentment with Him, His religion and His Messenger, this is a consequence of His love.

This is why the Prophet (PBUH) mentioned finding the taste of faith, as he mentioned about love feeling the sweetness of faith. The two authentic hadiths are foundational for the religious theistic passion and taste, and not the invented and misguided one. It is narrated in Sahih Muslim that the Prophet (PBUH) said: "*He has found the taste of faith—he who is content with Allah as his Lord, with Islam as his religion and with Muhammad (PBUH) as his Prophet.*" It is also stated in the Sahih books that the Prophet (PBUH) said: "*Whoever possesses the following three qualities will taste the sweetness [delight] of faith: to regard Allah and His Apostle as dearer than anything else, to love a person and love them only for Allah's sake, and to hate to revert to disbelief as one hates*

to be thrown into the fire. " This leads us to talk about love, so we say:

Love for Allah and His Messenger (PBUH)

Love for Allah, or rather Love for Allah and his Messenger is among the greatest obligations of faith, its major principles and its most significant foundations. Rather it is the foundation of every deed of the faith and the religion. Additionally, believing it is the foundation of every statement of the faith and the religion. **Every movement in existence stems from love**: either a praiseworthy love or an objectionable love. We have explained that in detail in "Qa'idat al-Mahabbah (A Base for Love)", among the major bases.

All the religious theistic deeds do not originate except from the praiseworthy love, and the origin of praiseworthy love is the love for Allah (the Exalted, the Majestic), as the deeds that arise from love that is detested by Allah is not a righteous deed. Rather all the religious theistic deeds do not arise except from the love for Allah, for Allah (the Exalted) does not accept of deeds except what is dedicated to him, as stated in the Sahih books, as narrated by the Prophet (PBUH) that He said: "***I am the Most Self-Sufficient and I have no need for an associate.***

Thus, he who does an deed for someone else's sake as well as Mine will have that action entirely renounced by Me to him whom he associated with Me."

It was stated in the Sahih that the first three with whom the fire will be enflamed are: **"the ostentatious reciter, the ostentatious fighter and the ostentatious philanthropist."**

Being sincere to Allah in religion is the only religion accepted by Allah, and it what he sent the earlier and later Messengers and sent all the books to preach, it is what the imams of faith agree upon, it is the summary of the Prophetic message and it is the center about which the Qur'an revolves.

Allah (the Exalted) said: "***{The revelation of this Book is from Allah—the Almighty, All-Wise. Indeed, We have sent down the Book to you O Prophet in truth, so worship Allah alone, being sincerely devoted to Him. Indeed, sincere devotion is due only to Allah ...}***" [39:1-3]. The majority of the Surah revolves about that concept, such as Allah's saying: "***{Say, [O Muhammad], "Indeed, I have been commanded to worship Allah, [being] sincere to Him in religion.}***" until His saying: "***{Say, "Allah [alone] do I worship, sincere to Him in my religion.}***" [39:11-14], as well as His saying: "***{Is not Allah sufficient for His***

Servant [i.e., Prophet Muhammad (PBUH)]? And [yet], they threaten you with those [they worship] other than Him. ...}" until His saying: *"{... ay, "Then have you considered what you invoke besides Allah? If Allah intended me harm, are they removers of His harm ...}"* [39:36-38], as well as His saying: *"{Or have they taken other than Allah as intercessors? Say, "Even though they do not possess [power over] anything, nor do they reason?" Say, "To Allah belongs [the right to allow] intercession entirely. To Him belongs the dominion of the heavens and the earth. Then to Him you will be returned." And when Allah is mentioned alone, the hearts of those who do not believe in the Hereafter shrink with aversion, but when those [worshipped] other than Him are mentioned, immediately they rejoice.}"* [38: 43-45], as well as His saying: *"{Say, [O Muhammad], "Is it other than Allah that you order me to worship, O ignorant ones?"}"* until His saying: *"{Rather, worship [only] Allah and be among the grateful.}"* [38:64-66].

Allah (the Exalted) said in the story of Adam (PBUH) and Iblis that Iblis said: *"{By Your might, I will surely mislead them all. Except, among them, Your chosen servants.}"* [38:82-83]. Allah (the Exalted) also said: *"{Indeed, My servants - no authority will you have over them, except those who follow you of the deviators.}*" [15:42]. He also said: "*{Indeed, there is for him no authority over those who have believed and rely upon their Lord. His authority is only over those who take him as an ally and those who through him associate others with Allah.}*" [16:99-100]. Therefore, Allah clarified that the power and seduction of Satan is only for the non-chosen, which is why He said in the story of Joseph (PBUH): "*{... And thus [it was] that We should avert from him evil and immorality. Indeed, he was of Our chosen servants.}*" [12:24]. The followers of Satan are the residents of Hellfire, as He (the Exalted) said: "*{[That] I will surely fill Hell with you and those of them that follow you all together."}*" [38:85].

He (the Exalted) also said: "*{Indeed, Allah does not forgive association with Him, but He forgives what is less than that for whom He wills ...}*" [4:48]. This verse addresses those who did not repent, which is why he specified association and restricted the other sins with His will. So, He informed that He does not forgive association for whoever did not repent therefrom, and he forgives what is less than it for whomever He wills. As for His saying: "*{Say, "O My servants who have transgressed against themselves [by sinning], do not despair of the mercy of Allah. Indeed, Allah forgives all sins ...}*"

[39:53], it addresses the repentant, which is why it is unspecified and unrestricted. The context of the verse, along with the cause of its revelation, clarify that.

He (the Exalted) outlined that the earlier and later nations were commanded to do that on multiple occasions, such as the Surah recited by the Prophet (PBUH) to Ubayy when Allah (the Exalted) commanded him to recite it to him specially, wherein Allah said: "**{Nor did those who were given the Scripture become divided until after there had come to them clear evidence. And they were not commanded except to worship Allah, [being] sincere to Him in religion, inclining to truth …}**" until the end of the verse [98:4-5].

This is the essence of the statement: "There is no deity except Allah," with which Allah sent all the Messengers. Allah (the Exalted) said: "**{And We sent not before you any messenger except We revealed to him that, "There is no deity except Me, so worship Me."}**" [21:25], and said: "**{And ask those We sent before you of Our messengers; have We made besides the Most Merciful deities to be worshipped?}**" [43:45], and said: "**{And We certainly sent into every nation a messenger, [saying], "Worship Allah and avoid Tāghūt (False objects of worship)."}**" [16:36].

All messengers opened their preaching with this foundational principle, as Noah (PBUH) said: "*{... **worship Allah; you have no deity other than Him ...**}*" [23:23]. Similarly, Hud, Salih, Shu'aib and others (PBUT) each said: "**worship Allah; you have no deity other than Him**", particularly the best among the Messengers, whom Allah took as intimate friends, Abraham and Muhammad (PBUT). This foundational principle was clarified by Allah through them, and He supported them therein and spread it with them. Abraham is the leader about whom Allah said: "*{... **Indeed, I will make you a leader for the people ...**}*" [2:124], and in his descendants, Allah placed the prophethood, scripture and message. The people of this prophethood and message are from his descendants whom Allah has blessed. He (the Exalted) said: "*{**And [mention, O Muhammad], when Abraham said to his father and his people, "Indeed, I am disassociated from that which you worship Except for He who created me; and indeed, He will guide me." And he made it a word remaining among his descendants that they might return [to it].**}*" [43:26-28].

This word is the word of devotion to Allah, and it is to renounce every worshipped being except the Creator who created us, as the man in Surah Ya-sin said: "*{**And why should I not worship***

He who created me and to whom you will be returned? Should I take other than Him [false] deities [while], if the Most Merciful intends for me some adversity, their intercession will not avail me at all, nor can they save me?}" [36:22-23]. Allah (the Exalted) said in the story of Abraham, after mentioning what clarifies the error of those who took some stars as a deity to be worshipped beside Allah, He said: "*{... But when it set, he said, "O my people, indeed I am free from what you associate with Allah. Indeed, I have turned my face [i.e., self] toward He who created the heavens and the earth, inclining toward truth, and I am not of those who associate others with Allah."}*" until His saying: "*{... while you do not fear that you have associated with Allah that for which He has not sent down to you any authority ...}*" [6:78-81]. Abraham (PBUH) said: "*{He said, "Then do you see what you have been worshipping, You and your ancient forefathers? Indeed, they are enemies to me, except the Lord of the worlds, Who created me, and He [it is who] guides me. And it is He who feeds me and gives me drink. And when I am ill, it is He who cures me And who will cause me to die and then bring me to life}*" [26:75-81]. Allah (the Exalted) also said: "*{There has already been for you an excellent pattern in Abraham and those with him, when they said to their people, "Indeed, we* are disassociated from you and from whatever you worship other than Allah …}" until the end of the verse [60:4].

Our Prophet (PBUH) is the one with whom Allah established His pure religion–the religion of Allah's Oneness, and suppressed the polytheists with him, both those who were polytheists originally and those who disbelieved among the People of the Scripture.

The Prophet (PBUH) said, as stated by Imam Ahmad and others: "*I was sent with the sword near the Hour [i.e., the Day of Judgment] so that Allah is worshipped alone, without a partner. He made my provision under the shadow of my spear, and He placed humility and degradation upon whoever goes against my command. He who imitates any people is considered to be one of them.*" We have already stated some of the verses that Allah revealed to him concerning His Oneness.

He (the Exalted) also said: "*{By those [angels] lined up in rows}*" until His saying: "*{Indeed, your God is One,}*" [37:1-4], and said: "*{Indeed they, when it was said to them, "There is no deity but Allah," were arrogant And were saying, "Are we to leave our gods for a mad poet?" Rather, he [i.e., the Prophet*

(PBUH)] has come with the truth and confirmed the [previous] messengers.}" until His saying: "**{Those will have a provision determined}**" [37:35-41], in addition to what He mentioned of the stories of Prophets in preaching Allah's Oneness and devoting the religion to Allah until His saying: "**{Exalted is Allah above what they describe, Except the chosen servants of Allah [who do not share in that sin].}**" [37:159-160]. Allah (the Exalted) also said: "**{Indeed, the hypocrites will be in the lowest depths of the Fire - and never will you find for them a helper - Except for those who repent, correct themselves, hold fast to Allah, and are sincere in their religion for Allah, for those will be with the believers. And Allah is going to give the believers a great reward.}**" [4:145-146].

In general, this foundational principle is frequent and evident in Surah al-An'am, al-A'raf, al-Nur[7], the Ta-Seen-Meem group of Surahs[8], the Ha-Meem group of Surahs[9], the Mufassal group of chapters[10] as well as other chapters that were revealed in Mecca and some that were revealed in Madinah. This is the principle of principles and the basis of the religion, even in the

---

[7] The 6th, 7th and 24th chapters of the Holy Qur'an, respectively.
[8] This term refers to chapters 26 to 28 of the Holy Qur'an.
[9] This term refers to chapters 39 to 46 of the Holy Qur'an
[10] This term refers to the relatively shorter chapters of the Holy Qur'an, namely from Surah Qaf (Chapter 50) until the end of the Mus'haf.

two Surahs of Ikhlas (Devotion): Surah al-Kafirun and Surah al-Ikhlas[11]. The Prophet used to recite these two chapters in the optional prayers, such as the prayer of Tawaf and the optional prayer before Dawn Prayer, and they both include Tawhid (the Oneness of Allah).

As for Surah al-Kafirun, it includes the practical and voluntary Tawhid, which is devoting the religion to Allah with the aim and will, which is what is mostly mentioned by the sheikhs of Sufism. As for Surah al-Ikhlas, it involves the verbal and practical Tawhid, as stated in the Sahih Books, from Aishah that a man used to always recite Surah al-Ikhlas in his prayer, so the Prophet (PBUH) said: *"**Ask him why he does so?**"* He was asked and he said: *"This Surah contains the Attributes of Allah, the Gracious, and I love to recite it."* The Messenger (PBUH) then told them: *"**Tell him that Allah loves him.**"*

Therefore, this Surah included descriptions of Allah (the Exalted, the Majestic) that contradict the allegations of the people of Ta'til[12] and the people of Tamthil[13], which made it

---

[11] The 109th and 112th chapters of the Holy Qur'an, respectively.
[12] Those who practice Ta'til (literally: suspension), which means the denial of some or all of the attributes of Allah.
[13] Those who practice Tamthil or Tashbih (literally: likening), which means likening Allah in His attributes to His creatures.

the authoritative reference in the Divine Entity issues, as we have explained in detail elsewhere.

We also mentioned how the Imams of jurisprudence rely on it with what is included therein of interpretation of the attributes of Allah: "the One and Indivisible" and "the Eternal Refuge", as was interpreted by the Prophet (PBUH), the Companions and the Followers, and the signs that indicate that.

However, the main point here is "the practical Tawhid", which means devoting the religion to Allah, although each kind is connected to the other. There is no one among the people of Ta'til (like the Juhamis) and the people of Tamthil except they have a form of practical association (polytheism). The root of their claims contains association and equating Allah to His creation, or equating Him to the nonexistent, as the people of Ta'til make Him equal to the nonexistent in the negative attributes that do not necessitate praise or affirmation of perfection. Alternatively, they make Him equal to the imperfect beings in the attributes of imperfection. And if they affirm the attributes, they and their counterparts of the people of Tamthil make Him equal to the creatures in their realities, so much so that they may worship them. Thus, they equate others with Allah and they attribute equals to Him.

The Jews often equate the Creator with the created and liken Him to it until they attribute, to Allah, helplessness, poverty, avarice and other deficiencies, from which He must be exalted, and which are the traits of His creatures.

On the other hand, the Christians often equate the created to the Creator until they attribute, to the creatures, attributes of Lordship and Divinity that is not befitting except for the Creator, exalted is He and high above what the wrongdoers say by great sublimity.

Allah (the Exalted, the Majestic) commanded us to ask Him to guide us to the straight path, the path of those upon whom He has bestowed favor, of the prophets, the steadfast affirmers of truth, the martyrs and the righteous, not of those who have earned His anger or of those who are astray. The Prophet (PBUH) said: *"The Jews have earned Allah's anger, and the Christians are astray."* There are some in this Ummah who hold resemblance with those and those, as the Prophet (PBUH) said: *"You will follow the ways of those nations who were before you, span by span and cubit by cubit (i.e., inch by inch) so much so that even if they entered a hole of a mastigure (a type of lizard), you would follow them."* They said: "O Allah's

Messenger! (Do you mean) the Jews and the Christians?" He said: **"Whom else?"** The hadith is stated in the Sahih books.

So, if the foundation of the religious deed is devoting the religion to Allah, which means desiring Allah alone, the object that is desired for itself is loved for itself, which is the utmost love. However, the requirement mostly came under the name of worshipping, such as His saying: "**{And I did not create the jinn and mankind except to worship Me.}**" [51:56], and His saying: "**{O mankind, worship your Lord, who created you and those before you …}**" [2:21], and the like. Worshipping includes perfect and utmost love and perfect and utmost humility. The loved one whose lover does not glorify him and humble himself before him is not worshipped, and the glorified one who is not loved is not worshipped. This is why Allah (the Exalted) said: "**{And [yet], among the people are those who take other than Allah as equals [to Him]. They love them as they [should] love Allah. But those who believe are stronger in love for Allah …}**" [2:165]. He (the Exalted) clarified that those who associate with their Lord, who take others as equal to Allah, even if they love them as they love Allah, the believers love Allah more than these polytheists love Allah and their idols, because the believers know Allah better, and love is contingent upon knowledge, and because the believers dedicated all their love to Allah alone, while these people assigned some of their love to others and associated others with Him in love. It is known that the former is a more perfect love. Allah (the Exalted) said: "*{Allah presents an example: a man [i.e., slave] owned by quarreling partners and another belonging exclusively to one man - are they equal in comparison? Praise be to Allah! But most of them do not know.}*" [39:29].

The term 'love' is unrestricted and unspecified, for the believer loves Allah, loves His messengers, prophets and righteous servants, although that is derived from the love for Allah. However, the love that is for Allah is not deserved by anyone else. That is why the love for Allah (the Exalted, the Majestic) was mentioned with what is exclusive for Him of worshipping, repentance, devotion and so on. All these terms include the love for Allah (the Exalted, the Majestic).

He also clarified that loving Him is the foundation of the religion, as He showed that the religion becomes perfect with its perfectness and deficient with its deficiency. The Prophet (PBUH) said: "**The root (foundation) of this matter is Islam, its pillar (mainstay) is the prayer and its highest point is Jihad (fighting in the Cause of Allah).**" Thereupon, he informed that

Jihad is the highest and most honorable deed. Allah (the Exalted) said: "*{Have you made the providing of water for the pilgrim and the maintenance of al-Masjid al-Ḥarām equal to [the deeds of] one who believes in Allah and the Last Day and strives in the cause of Allah? They are not equal in the sight of Allah …}*" until His saying: "*{… a great reward.}*" [9:19-22]. The texts regarding the virtues of Jihad and its people are abundant.

It is affirmed that it is the best thing with which the servant can volunteer. Jihad is the proof of perfect love. Allah (the Exalted) said: "*{Say, O Prophet, "If your parents and children and siblings and spouses and extended family …}*" until the end of the verse [9:24]. He also said about the qualities of the lovers and loved ones: "*{O you who have believed, whoever of you should revert from his religion - Allah will bring forth [in place of them] a people He will love and who will love Him [who are] humble toward the believers, strong against the disbelievers; they strive in the cause of Allah and do not fear the blame of a critic …}*" [5:54]. He described the lovers and loved ones that they are humble towards the believers, strong against the disbelievers, and that they strive in the cause of Allah and do not fear the blame of a critic.

Love necessitates Jihad, for the lover loves what his loved one loves and hates what he hates, he allies himself with the allies of his loved one and shows animosity to his enemies, he becomes pleased at the pleasure of his loved one and displeased at his displeasure, and he commands what his loved one commands and forbids what he forbids, so he conforms with his loved one in this regard. Those are the ones at whose pleasure Allah becomes pleased, and at whose displeasure Allah becomes displeased, because they become pleased at His pleasure and displeased at His displeasure. The Prophet (PBUH) said to Abu Bakr about a group of Companions that included Suhaib and Bilal: **"O Abu Bakr, perhaps you have angered them. If so, you have angered your Lord."** Abu Bakr said to them: *"O brothers! Have I offended you?"* They said: *"No. May Allah forgive you, O Abu Bakr!"* The context for this is that Abu Sufian ibn Harb had passed by them, so they said: *"The swords of Allah did not exact their due from the foes of Allah."* So, Abu Bakr said to them: *"Do you speak like that to the chief of Quraish?"* and when Abu Bakr mentioned this to the Prophet (PBUH) he said the aforementioned statement, because those people said what they did out of anger for Allah's sake, due to their perfect alliance for the allies of Allah and His Messenger, and animosity to the enemies of Allah and His Messenger.

This is why the Prophet (PBUH) said in the authentic hadith which he narrates from His Lord: "*… and My servant keeps on coming closer to Me through performing Nawafil (non-obligatory good deeds) till I love him. When I love him, I become his sense of hearing with which he hears, and his sense of sight with which he sees, and his hand with which he grips, and his leg with which he walks; and if he asks Me, I will give him, and if he asks My protection, I will protect him; and I do not hesitate to do anything as I hesitate to take the soul of the believer, for he hates death, and I hate to disappoint him, but there is no escaping it.*"" He (the Exalted) showed that He hesitates, because hesitation is the conflict of two wills: He (the Exalted) loves what His servant loves and hates what he hates; the servant hates death, so Allah hates it, as He said: "*and I hate to disappoint him,*" while He (the Exalted) decreed death, so He wants the servant to die. So, He called this a hesitation, and then He clarified that there is no escaping it.

but for Muslim scholars in it two sayings..

• CHAPTER 10 •

Confuting al-Hululiyyah[14]

This is agreement and unity in what is loved, approved and commanded and what is despised, disapproved and forbidden. It may be called specific or qualitative unity, but this is not unity of the two beings, for such is impossible, and whoever proclaims it is a heretic. This is the view of the Christians, the majority of Rafida and ascetics, such as al-Hallajis and others, which is **the restricted unity** in something specific.

As for **the absolute unity** which is the view of the people of the Unity of Existence, who claim that the existence of the created is the same thing as the existence of the creator, this is suspension and denial of the Creator, and it combines every type of association. As there are two types of unity, there are two types of Hulul (incarnation) as well: some people proclaim

---

[14] This term refers to those who believe in al-Hulul (incarnation).

Hulul that is restricted in some individuals, while others proclaim Hulul in everything, who are the Juhamis who say that the essence of Allah is everywhere.

Some people of Fanaa'[15] who are infatuated in love, may think they are obscured by their loved one from their own selves and love, and overshadowed by his remembrance from their own remembrance, with his knowledge from their own knowledge, and with his existence from their own existence, until they can only perceive their loved one, so one of them thinks, in his lack of awareness, deficiency of reason and intoxication of love, that he himself is his loved one. It was said that a loved one fell in the river, so the lover threw himself after the loved one, who said: "*I fell, so why did you fall?*" He said: "*I am obscured by you from myself, so I thought that I am you.*" Undoubtedly, this is error and aberration.

However, if this is due to the strength of love and remembrance and not because of a prohibited cause that led to the demise of his intellect, he is excused for the demise of his intellect, and he is not held accountable for the words that come out of his mouth in this state where his intellect is gone

---

[15] Fanaa' in Sufism is the "passing away" or "annihilation" of the self. It means "to die before one dies".

without any prohibited cause. As was said about the wise among the insane: that they are people whom Allah granted intellects and states, so He took away their intellects and left them with their states, and He acquit them of what He had imposed for what He took away.

Nevertheless, if the cause that led to the demise of the intellect is prohibited, the intoxication is not excused, although he is not judged to be a heretic according to the stronger view, nor does his divorce take effect according to the stronger view, but the debate in the judgment is well-known.

We have spoken in detail about that and about whosoever state remains sound for him and whosoever does not in that "Base".

In any case the Fanaa' that leads one to such a state is a deficient state, although such a person is not held to account. This is why no such thing was narrated about the Companions, who are the best of this Ummah, nor about our Prophet Muhammad (PBUH), who is the best messenger. Although these people cling to the incident of the shocking of Moses (PBUH). However, the demise of the intellect began to happen upon the reception of Divine Warids[16] by some of the Followers and those who came after them.

If complete love necessitates conforming to the loved one in what he loves and hates, and whom he befriends and antagonizes, it is known that whoever loves Allah the due love must despise His enemies, and must love what He loves of fighting them, as He (the Exalted) said: "**{Indeed, Allah loves those who fight in His cause in a row as though they are a [single] structure joined firmly.}**" [61:4].

The utmost lover is not affected by the blame of critics. Rather this entices him to adhere to love, as most poets said in this regard. These are the people of praiseworthy blame, who do not fear to be blamed about what Allah loves and approves of struggling against His enemies, for many are criticized for this. As for those who are blamed for doing what Allah dislikes or neglecting what He loves, this is true blame, and it is not praiseworthy to endure such blame. Rather going back to the truth is better than persistence in falsehood. This is how distinction is made between the blamed ones who do what Allah and His Messenger love without fearing the blame of critics therein, and between the blamed ones who do what Allah and His Messenger dislike and endure blame therein.

---

[16] In Sufism, Warid is the effect of practicing dhikr and wird on the heart of the practicer.

Fear and Hope and Confuting those who Allege they Worship but not out of Longing to His Paradise or Fear of His Hellfire

If love is the foundation of every religious deed, fear, hope and other matters require love and stem from it. The hopeful and desirous desires what he loves, and not what he hates, and the fearful flees what he fears to attain what he loves. Allah (the Exalted) said: "*{Those whom they invoke seek means of access to their Lord, [striving as to] which of them would be nearest, and they hope for His mercy and fear His punishment ...}*" until the end of the verse [17:57], and said: "*{Indeed, those who have believed and those who have emigrated and fought in the cause of Allah - those expect the mercy of Allah. And Allah is Forgiving and Merciful.}*" [2:218].

His mercy is a term that combines every good thing, and **His punishment** is a term that combines every evil. **The place of pure mercy** is Paradise while **the place of pure punishment** is Hellfire. As for **the worldly life**, it is a place of mixture. Hope, even if it was related to entering Paradise, it combines every pleasure, the highest of which is gazing at the Face of Allah, as stated in Sahih Muslim from Thabit, from Abdurrahman ibn

Layla, from Suhaib, that the Prophet (PBUH) said: **"When the people of Paradise enter Paradise, and the people of Hellfire enter Hellfire, a caller will cry out: "O people of Paradise! You have a covenant with Allah and He wants to fulfill it." They will say: "What is it? Has Allah not made our faces bright, and made the Balance (of our good deeds) heavy, and admitted us to Paradise and saved us from Hellfire?" Then the Veil will be lifted and they will look upon Him, and by Allah, Allah will not give them anything that is more beloved to them or delightful, than looking upon Him."** This is the extra[17].

This removes the uncertainty about the statement: "*I did not worship You out of longing for Your Paradise or fear of Your Hellfire, but rather out of longing to seeing You.*" The person who made this statement and those who agree with him thought that the term: 'Paradise' only includes food, drinks, clothing, [sexual] pleasure, hearing and other forms of enjoyment with creatures. In this regard, they are in agreement with those who deny seeing Allah of the Juhamis, or those who affirm it but claim there is no pleasure in the act of seeing Allah, as a group of jurisprudence learners said. All of those agree that

---

[17] In reference to verse [10:26] of the Holy Qur'an, wherein Allah says: "***{For them who have done good is the best [reward] - and extra ...}***".

the terms: 'Paradise' and 'the Hereafter' do not include except enjoyment with the creatures. This is why some mistaken sheikh said when he heard Allah's saying: "*{... Among you are some who desire this world, and among you are some who desire the Hereafter ...}*" [3:152], so he said: "*So where are those who desire Allah?*" Another said about Allah's saying: "*{Indeed, Allah has purchased from the believers their lives and their properties [in exchange] for that they will have Paradise ...}*" [9:111], so he said: "*If the lives and the properties are in exchange for Paradise, so where is looking at Him?*" All this is due to their thinking that Paradise does not include looking at Him.

The correct notion is that Paradise is the place that combines every pleasure, and the highest of which is looking at the Face of Allah, which is among the pleasure that they attain in Paradise, as the texts inform. Similarly, the people of Hellfire are partitioned from their Lord and they enter Hellfire. However, if the one who said such statement was aware of what he said, he meant: "*Even if You had not created Hellfire or Paradise, You would have also been worthy of worshipping, endearment and observation.*" What he means by Paradise here is the place where the creature enjoys.

As for the person's deeds without love or even will, this is impossible, even if some mistaken ascetics imagined it and thought that utmost servitude is to have no will at all. This is because if he speaks about Fanaa' and the one who practices it – who is preoccupied with his loved one – he has a will and love, but he does not feel them. The existence of love and will is one thing, and feeling them is another thing. But when they could not feel it, they thought it does not exist, which is a mistake. The servant cannot behave except out of love, hate and will. This is why the Prophet (PBUH) said: *"The truest names are Harith (Harvester) and Hammam (Determined)."* Every person has a harvest, which is his deeds, and has a determination, which is the foundation of will. However, sometimes the heart contains of the love for Allah what invites the person to obey Him, and of glorification and shyness of Allah what prevents the person from disobeying Him. Umar ibn al-Khattab said: *"What a good servant [of Allah] Suhaib is! [Even] if he did not fear Allah, he would not disobey him,"* meaning that he did not disobey Allah even if he did not fear Him, so how about if he did? His glorification and veneration of Allah prevent him from disobeying Him.

If the fear and hope of **the hopeful and fearful** pertain to punishment by the Lord being obscured from him, and pleasure with the Lord being revealed to him, it is known that this is a consequence of his love for Him. Love is what caused the love for revelation and fear of obscurement. And if his fear and hope pertain to punishment and enjoyment with a created being, he can only pursue that through the worshipping of Allah, which necessitates loving Him. Then, if he finds the sweetness of Allah's love, he will find it sweeter than any other love. This is why the residents of Paradise are more preoccupied with that than anything else. The hadith states: "**The residents of Paradise will be inspired to exalt Allah as easily as they breathe,**" which shows their utmost pleasure with the exaltation and love of Allah. Fear of punishment with a created being and hope for pleasure with the same leads to the love for Allah, which is the foundation.

All this is based on **the foundation of love**, and the Book and the Sunnah have spoken about the love of the believing servants, as in Allah's saying: "**{... But those who believe are stronger in love for Allah ...}**" [2:165], His saying: "**{... a people He will love and who will love Him ...}**" [5:54], and His saying: "**{... are more beloved to you than Allah and His Messenger** *and jihād [i.e., striving] in His cause ...}*" [9:24]. It is stated in the Sahih books that the Prophet (PBUH) said: "**Whoever possesses the following three qualities will taste the sweetness [delight] of faith: to regard Allah and His Apostle as dearer than anything else, to love a person and love them only for Allah's sake, and to hate to revert to disbelief as one hates to be thrown into the fire.**"

Rather the love for the Messenger (PBUH) became necessary due to the love for Allah (the Exalted), as in His saying: "*{... are more beloved to you than Allah and His Messenger ...}*" [9:24], and as in the Sahih Books that the Prophet (PBUH) said: "**None of you believes till I am dearer to him than his father, his child, and all mankind.**" It is also stated in Sahih al-Bukhari that Umar ibn al-Khattab said: "*O Allah's Messenger (PBUH)! You are dearer to me than everything except my own self.*" The Prophet (PBUH) said: "**No, O Umar, (you will not have complete faith) till I am dearer to you than your own self.**" Then Umar said to him: "*However, now, by Allah, you are dearer to me than my own self.*" The Prophet (PBUH) said: "**Now, O Umar, (now you are a believer).**"

Similarly, the love for his Companions and relatives, as stated in the Sahih Books that the Prophet (PBUH) said: "**Love for the**

Ansar is a sign of faith and hatred for the Ansar is a sign of hypocrisy.*" He also said: "**The person who believes in Allah and the Last Day never nurses a grudge against the Ansar.**" Ali (may Allah be pleased with him) said: "**The illiterate Messenger (PBUH) gave me a promise that no one but a believer would love me, and none but a hypocrite would nurse grudge against me.**" It is stated in the Sunan that he (PBUH) said to al-Abbas: "**By Him in whose hand my soul is, they shall not enter Paradise until they love you (i.e., the Messenger's relatives) for the sake of Allah and for your kinship to me.**" A hadith is narrated by Ibn Abbas and attributed to the Prophet (PBUH) that he said: "**Love Allah for what He nourishes you with of His Blessings, love me due to the love of Allah, and love the people of my house due to love of me.**"

As for the love of the Almighty Lord for His servant, Allah (the Exalted) said: "*{... And Allah took Abraham as an intimate friend.}*" [4:125], He said: "*{... a people He will love and who will love Him ...}*" [5:54], He said: "*{... And do good; indeed, Allah loves the doers of good.}*" [2:195], He said: "*{... so complete for them their treaty until their term [has ended]. Indeed, Allah loves the righteous [who fear Him].}*" [9:4], "*{So as long as they are upright toward you, be upright toward* *them. Indeed, Allah loves the righteous [who fear Him].}"* [9:7], *"{Indeed, Allah loves those who fight in His cause in a row as though they are a [single] structure joined firmly.}"* [61:4], *"{But yes, whoever fulfills his commitment and fears Allah - then indeed, Allah loves those who fear Him.}"* [3:76].

As for the deeds that are loved by Allah of the apparent and concealed compulsory and optional deeds, they are many and well-known, as well as His love for its doers, who are the believing and Godfearing allies of Allah.

This love is a truth, as spoken by the Book and the Sunnah. It is the consensus of the early Muslims and scholars, the people of the Sunnah and Hadith, all the followed religious sheikhs and the leaders of Sufism, that Allah (the Exalted) is loved for Himself a true love, or rather the most perfect love – as He (the Exalted) said: "*{... But those who believe are stronger in love for Allah ...}*" [2:165] – and that He (the Exalted) loves His believing servants a true love as well.

The Juhamis denied the truth about the reciprocating love, alleging that love does not occur without a relation between the lover and the loved one, and that there is no relation between the Eternal and the created that would necessitate love. The first one to invent this in Islam is **al-Ja'ad ibn Dirham** in the early second century, so Khalid ibn Abdullah al-Qasry, the governor of Iraq and the East, sacrificed him in Wasit. He delivered a sermon to the people on the day of al-Adha and said: *"O people! Offer your sacrifices, may Allah accept them from you. I shall sacrifice al-Ja'ad ibn Dirham. He alleged that Allah did not take Abraham as an intimate friend and did not speak to Moses directly."* Then, he got down and slaughtered him. This notion was taken from him by **al-Jaham ibn Safwan**, so he spread it and defended it in debates, and the Jahami belief was attributed to him, so Salam ibn Ahwaz, the governor of Khorasan killed him. After that, this view moved to the Mutazilites, the followers of Amr ibn Ubaid, and their voice became heard during the reign of al-Ma'mun, until the Imams of Islam were tried and invited to concord with them on that.

This statement of theirs originated from the polytheists, the Sabians of Brahmin, philosophers and the heretics of the People of the Scripture, who allege that the Lord has no affirmative attributes at all. These are the enemies of Abraham (PBUH), who worship stars, build temples for the stars and so on, and they deny, in fact, that Abraham is a Khalil (intimate friend) of Allah and that Moses is a Kalim (converser) with

Allah, because intimate friendship is the perfect love that dominates the lover, as was said:

She penetrated my soul	Which is how 'Khalil'[18] got its name

This is proven by what is stated in the Sahih Books, as narrated by Abu Saied, that the Prophet (PBUH) said: **"If I were to choose an intimate friend, I would have definitely chosen Abu Bakr as my intimate friend, but Allah, the Exalted and Glorious. has taken your brother and companion (meaning Prophet himself) as a friend."** In another version, he said: **"I stand acquitted before Allah that I took any one of you as an intimate friend and if I were to choose anyone as an intimate friend, I would have taken Abu Bakr as my intimate friend."** In another version, he said: **"Allah has taken me as an intimate friend, just as he had taken Abraham as an intimate friend."** Thus, he (PBUH) clarified that he must no take mortals as friends, but if he had been able to, the worthiest among the people would have been Abu Bakr.

---

[18] The word 'Khalil' (intimate friend) and the word 'Takhallal' (to penetrate) are derived from the same origin.

However, he (PBUH) described himself that he loves some people, as he said to Mu'adh: "**By Allah, I love you,**" and similarly what he said to Ansar as well. Zaid ibn Harithah was the sweetheart of the Messenger (PBUH), and so was his son Usamah, and there many other examples. Amr ibn al-Aas said to him: "*Who is the most beloved to you among the people?*" He said: "**Aishah.**" He said: "*And among the men?*" He said: "**Her father (Abu Bakr).**" The Messenger (PBUH) also said to his daughter, Fatimah: "**Don't you love what I love?**" She said: "*I do!*" He said: "**So, love Aishah.**". The Messenger (PBUH) also said to al-Hasan: "**O Allah! I love him, so love him and love whoever loves him.**" There are many such examples.

Therefore, he described himself that he loves certain people while he said: "**I stand acquitted before Allah that I took any one of you as an intimate friend and if I were to choose anyone as an intimate friend, I would have taken Abu Bakr as my intimate friend.**" So, intimate friendship is more specific than general love, for because of its perfectness and penetration of the lover, the loved one becomes loved for himself, and not for anything else. What is loved for something else is subsequent to that thing in love. However, due to the perfectness of intimate friendship, it does not accept partnership or competition, as it penetrates the lover, **so it contains perfect Tawhid and perfect love.**

Intimate friendship contradicts rivalry and the precedence of others, so that the loved one is loved for himself a love that is unrivaled by any other. Such love is fit only for Allah, as no one else must share with Him in the love that He deserves. He is loved for Himself, and everything else that is loved – if it is truly loved – is loved for His own sake. As for everything that is loved for the sake of someone else, such love is false; the worldly life is cursed and everything in it is cursed except what is for the sake of Allah (the Exalted). If this is how intimate friendship is, then it is a given that whoever denies that Allah is loved for Himself also denies His intimate friendship. Similarly, the person who denies that Allah loves any of His servants also denies that He would take an intimate friend to love Him and be loved by Him in the most perfect way that is fit for the creatures.

Similarly, they denied His conversing with Moses because they deny that any attribute or action is established in Him. As they deny that he would have the attributes of life, power or knowledge, or to be established or to come, they also deny that He speaks or be spoken to. This is the essence of their claim,

"{... Thus spoke those before them like their words. Their hearts resemble each other ...}" [2:118].

And since Islam is widespread and the Qur'an is recited everywhere and cannot be denied by anyone who declares Islam, they began practicing deviation concerning the names of Allah and distort words from their proper place. So, they interpreted the servants' love for Him to be merely their love for worshipping Him or becoming closer to Him, which is great ignorance. The love for becoming closer to someone is a consequence of the love for him. Whoever does not love something cannot love becoming close to it. Becoming closer is a means, and the love for the means is a consequence of the love for the end. Therefore, the means to the end cannot be the object of love without the end itself.

Similarly, concerning worshipping and obedience, if it said regarding the worshipped and obeyed: this person loves obeying and worshipping him, such love stems from the love for the person himself. Otherwise, if he does not love him, he will not love worshipping and obeying him. The person who does not work for another except for a recompense that he takes from him or to avoid a punishment becomes a compensator or redeemer and not a lover, and it cannot be said that this person loves him and interpret that love as love for his obedience and worshipping. If love for the end requires love for the means or lack of love for the means, this necessitates expressing **the love for work as love for compensation or redemption. As for the love for Allah**, it does not pertain merely to the **love for compensation**. If someone hired a worker for a fee, it is not said that the worker loves him merely for that. One may hire a worker that he does not like at all, but rather hates. Similarly, a person who redeems himself, with an action, from the punishment of a punisher, it is not said that he loves him, for he may hate him. Therefore, Allah's description for the believers that they love Him cannot be merely love for the deeds with which they attain some created rewards without loving their lord in the first place.

In addition, the term 'worshipping' includes love with humility as mentioned before, This is why human love has various stages.

First: **Attachment:** the heart's attachment to the loved one, then there is **longing:** the pouring out of the heart to him, then there is **passion:** which is inseparable love, then **amorousness**, and the final stage is **infatuation**, which is worshipping of the loved one. The lover's heart remains in remembrance, worshipping and humbleness for his loved one.

Moreover, the term 'repentance to him' also necessitates love, and so does the similar terms, as previously mentioned.

In addition, if what they said were true, that [i.e., the verses that speak about love for Allah] would be figurative speech due to the omission and concealment therein, and the figurative speech cannot be put forth without the context that shows the intended meaning.

It is known that there is nothing in the Book of Allah or the Sunnah of His Messenger to deny that Allah is loved and prove that nothing is loved except the deeds themselves, neither the connected nor the separate connotations indicate that, nor does the intellect. Among the signs of figurative speech, is the validity of its negative, meaning that the statement that Allah does not love and is not loved must be valid, as their leader al-Ja'ad ibn Dirham proclaimed that Allah did not take Abraham as an intimate friend nor did He speak to Moses directly. However, it is established that this is impossible as per the consensus of Muslims. Therefore, the connotation of the consensus is that this is not figurative speech, but literal.

In addition, **Allah made distinction between loving Him and loving working for His sake** in His saying: "*{... are more beloved to you than Allah and His Messenger and jihād [i.e., striving] in His cause ...}*" [9:24], just as He made distinction between love for Him and love for His Messenger in the phrase "*{... are more beloved to you than Allah and His Messenger ...}*" If what is meant by love for Him is nothing more than love for the deeds, this would be repetition, or coupling of the specific with the general, both of which are against the apparent meaning and cannot be accepted except with a context that shows the intended meaning.

Just as love for Him cannot be interpreted merely as love for His Messenger, it cannot be interpreted merely as love for working for His sake, even if love for Him entails love for His Messenger and love for working for His sake.

Moreover, using the love for something to express merely the love for obeying it and not the love for it is not known in the language, literally or figuratively. Therefore, interpreting the statements as such is pure distortion. We have proved in multiple instances in 'the Major Bases' that none other than Allah cannot be loved and desired for himself, just as none other than Allah cannot exist by himself. On the contrary, there is no Lord except Allah and there is no deity except Allah. He is the deity that deserve to be loved for Himself and glorified for Himself with the utmost love and glorification.

"**Every newborn is born to the true nature.**" He (the Exalted) created the hearts so that they can find no peace and tranquility with what they love and desire except with Allah alone, and that with everything the person loves, of what is eaten, worn, seen, heard or touched, he will find that his heart desires something else, and loves a different thing, which he deifies, in which he seeks refuge and with which he feels reassured, and he observes what is like him of these races. This is why Allah (the Exalted) said in His Book: "*{... Unquestionably, by the remembrance of Allah hearts are assured.}*" [13:28]. It is authentically narrated by Iyadh ibn Himar, from the Prophet (PBUH), that Allah (the Exalted) said: "*... have created My servants as one having a natural inclination to the worship of Allah but it is Satan who turns them away from the right religion and he makes unlawful what has been declared lawful for them and he commands them to ascribe partnership with Me, although he has no justification for that ...*" It is also stated in the Sahih Books, as narrated by Abu Hurairah, that the Prophet (PBUH) said: "**Every child is born as a Muslim (i.e. with** *a natural inclination to worship none but Allah Alone) and his parents convert him to Judaism or Christianity or Magianism, as an animal delivers a perfect baby animal; do you find it mutilated?"* Then Abu Hurairah added: *"Recite, if you will, Allah's saying: "{... [Adhere to] the fiṭrah[19] of Allah upon which He has created [all] people. No change should there be in the creation of Allah. That is the correct religion ...}" [30:30]."*

In addition, for all the attributes of perfection that the hearts are inclined to love, Allah is the one who is worthy of them in their perfect form, and every quality that is loved in anyone beside Him comes from Him (the Exalted, the Majestic), so He is the one who is worthy to be loved truly and perfectly. Denying the servant's love for his Lord is in fact a denial for His being a worshipped deity. Moreover, denying His love for His servant necessitates denying His will, which necessitates denying His being a Creator Lord. Therefore, denying that [i.e., His love for His servants] necessitates denying that He is the Lord of all beings and the Deity of all beings, which is the proclamation of the people of Ta'til and apostasy.

---

[19] The natural inborn inclination of man to worship his Creator prior to the corruption of his nature by external influences.

That is why the two nations that preceded us agreed, with the heritage and wisdom that they have from Moses and Jesus (PBUT), that the greatest commandment is to love Allah with all your heart, mind and intention, which is the essence of Hanifism, the religion of Abraham, which is the origin of the Sharia of the Torah, the Bible and the Qur'an. Such denial is borrowed from the polytheists and the Sabian–the enemies of Abraham, and those who concord with that view among the philosophers, theologians, jurisprudence learners and innovators in the religion, they borrowed it from those people. This arose in the Qarmatians of esotericism among the Isma'ilis. This is why the Khalil and the Imam of the Hanifis (PBUH) said: "*{... Then do you see what you have been worshipping, You and your ancient forefathers? Indeed, they are enemies to me, except the Lord of the worlds.}*" [26:75-77]. He also said: "*{I like not those that set [i.e., disappear].}*" [6:76], and also said: "*{The Day when there will not benefit [anyone] wealth or children but only one who comes to Allah with a sound heart.}*" [26:88-89], sound here mean sound from association.

As for their statement: "There is no relation between the created and the Eternal to entail loving Him and enjoying looking at Him," such statement is abstract. If by 'relation' they mean that there is no blood relation between them, this is true, and if they mean they do not have a relation like that which exists between the married parties or between the eater and the eaten, this is also true. However, if they mean that they do not have a relation to make one of them a loving worshipper and the other a loved and worshipped one, this is the premise of their argument, and using that as an argument is a 'begging the question' fallacy, which is sufficient to refute it.

One can respond by saying: Rather, there is no relation to necessitate complete love except the relation between the created and the Creator, except whom there is no deity, who is the only deity in the heaven and on the earth, and to whom belongs the highest description [i.e., attribute] in the heavens and earth. The essence of these people's claim is denying that Allah is truly worshipped. This is why some groups of theologian Sufis, who deny that Allah loves in fact, support that claim. They affirm Him being loved but deny Him being a lover, because they became Sufis while believing the statement of those theologians, so they took the Sufist belief in love, although they may be confused about it. The root of such denial is the claims of the Mutazilites and the Juhamis. As for the Lord's love for His servant, they deny that more fiercely. **Those who deny it are classified into two groups:**

(A group) that interpret it with the same actions that the servant loves, making Allah's love the same as the love of His creatures.

And (a group) that make it the same as His will for those actions. We have explained this in detail in "Qawa'id al-Sifat wal-Qadar (Rules of Attributes and Predestination)", and this is not the right place for it.

It is known that the Book, the Sunnah and the consensus of the early Muslims show that Allah loves and approves what He commanded doing, both compulsory and optional, even if that did not exist, and that He may will the existence of things and deeds that He despises and disapproves, such as defiance and disbelief. Allah (the Exalted) said: "*{And Allah does not like corruption.}*" [2:205], and said: "*{And He does not approve for His servants disbelief.}*" [39:7].

What is meant here is to mention the servants' love for their Deity.

• CHAPTER 11 •

Qur'anic Hearing and Satanic Hearing

This was shown to be the foundations for the acts of faith, and no one among the early Muslims, of Companions or Followers, was known to dispute that. They stirred this love with what Allah ordained to stir it, such as theistic knowledge and Qur'anic hearing. Allah (the Exalted) said: "***{And thus We have revealed to you an inspiration of Our command [i.e., the Qur'ān]. You did not know what is the Book or [what is] faith ...}***" until the end of the Surah [42:52-53].

Moreover, as the times passed, some who deny this love appeared amidst the theologian sects, such as Mutazilites and others.

And some appeared, amidst Sufis, who seek its stirring with things like hearing speech such as Taghbir [a type of singing] and hearing whistling and handclapping. So, they hear the speeches and poetry that stir love as a category, which stirs the love that lies in each heart, so it is as fit for the lover of idols, crosses, brethren, homeland, tyrants and women as it is for the lover of the Most Merciful. However, for the sheikhs they used to bring, they used to have requirements for the place, the possibility and the companions, and perhaps they required the sheikh that guards from the devil. Then, others went further in that until they ended up doing types of sins, or even wickedness. Some even ended up committing explicit apostasy, by experiencing the poems that contain disbelief and atheism, which is among the greatest corruption, and it produces states for them accordingly, just as the worshipping of the polytheists and the People of the Scripture worshippers produce for them.

The view of the scrutinizing sheikhs is, **as al-Junaid (may Allah be merciful to him) said**: *"Whoever intends to hear is tempted by it, and whoever happens to hear finds comfort in it."* This means that it is not ordained to gather for this invented hearing, and it must not be commanded or regarded as a religious deed or a means of closeness to Allah, for the means of closeness and worshipping are learned from the Messengers (PBUT), as there is nothing forbidden except what Allah forbade, and no religion except what Allah ordained.

Allah (the Exalted) said: "*{Or have they partners [i.e., other deities] who have ordained for them a religion to which Allah has not consented?}*" [42:21], and said: "*{Say, [O Muhammad], "If you should love Allah, then follow me, [so] Allah will love you and forgive you your sins ...}*" [3:31]. So, He made their love for Allah necessitate following His Messenger, and made their following of the Messenger (PBUH) necessitate Allah's love for them.

Precious Words of Ubayy ibn Ka'ab (may Allah be pleased with him)

Ubayy ibn Ka'ab (may Allah be pleased with him) said: "Adhere to the path and the Sunnah, for no servant who adheres to the path and the Sunnah mentions Allah and his skin shivers out of fear of Allah except his sins fall off him like the dry leaves fall off the tree, and no servant who adheres to the path and the Sunnah mentions Allah alone and his eyes tear out of fear of Allah except he is never touched by Hellfire. Verily, *moderation while following the path of the Sunnah is better than diligence while deviating from them. Thus, make sure you exercise moderation and diligence in your deeds while following the path of the Prophets and their Sunnah."* This is explained in detail elsewhere.

If the aforementioned [i.e., Taghbir and so on] were among what is commanded, recommended and fit to reform the hearts for the worshipped and loved one, the Sharia evidence would point to that. However, it is known that there was not among the three Preferred Generations – about which the Prophet (PBUH) said: **"The best of my Ummah is the generation among whom I was sent, then those who follow them, then those who follow them."** – neither in the Hijaz, in the Levant, in Yemen, in Iraq, in Egypt nor in Khorasan, anyone of righteousness and religion who used to go for this invented hearing to reform the hearts. This is why it was disapproved by the Imams of jurisprudence, such as Imam Ahmad and others, so much so that al-Shafi'y regarded it as the invention of heretics when he said: *"I left behind in Baghdad something invented by the heretics they call 'Taghbir', with which they avert people from the Holy Quran."*

As for the hearing that the person does not intend, no prohibition or criticism arise therefrom as per the consensus of the Imams. Praise and criticism arise from listening and not hearing. The person who listens to the Holy Qur'an is rewarded for that, while the one who hears it without intention or will is not rewarded for that, as the rewards of deeds are according to their intention. Similarly, for the amusements that are forbidden to listen to, if the person hears them unintentionally, no harm befalls him. If one hears a verse of poetry fits his state, stirring the praiseworthy dormant thing in him and agitating the desirable that resides in his heart or bringing it to his mind and so on, this is not forbidden. The praiseworthy and desirable here is the movement of his heart, which is loved by Allah and His Messenger, toward love for Allah, which entails doing what Allah loves and leaving what Allah hates. For example, the man who passed by a house and heard someone say:

Every day you change color	***Not doing that is more befitting of you***

So, he took from that a sign that fits his state. Sings fall under the category of analogy, consideration and setting examples.

The 'hearing' issue is large and prevalent, and we have talked about it elsewhere.

The point here is that the desirable aims of Murids are attained through **the theistic Qur'anic Prophetic religious lawful listening**, which is the listening of the Prophets, the listening of the people of knowledge, the listening of the acquainted, and the listening of the believers. Allah (the Exalted) said: "**{Those were the ones upon whom Allah bestowed favor from among the prophets of the descendants of Adam ...}**" until His saying: "**{... When the verses of the Most Merciful were recited to them, they fell in prostration and weeping.}**" [19:58]. He (the Exalted) also said: "**{... Indeed, those who were given knowledge before it - when it is recited to them, they fall upon their faces in prostration}**" until His saying: "**{... and it [i.e., the Qur'ān] increases them in humble submission.**" [17:107-109]. He (the Exalted) also said: "**{And when they hear what has been revealed to the Messenger, you see their eyes overflowing with tears because of what they have recognized of the truth ...}**" [5:83]. He also said: "**{The believers are only those who, when Allah is mentioned, their hearts become fearful, and when His verses are recited to them, it increases them in faith; and upon their Lord they rely.}**" [8:2].

He (the Exalted) said: "*{Allah has sent down the best statement: a consistent Book wherein is reiteration. The skins shiver therefrom of those who fear their Lord ...}*" until the end of the verse [39:23].

Just as He praised those who undertake such listening, he vilified those who turn away from it, as in His saying: "*{And of the people is he who buys the amusement of speech to mislead [others] from the way of Allah without knowledge and who takes it [i.e., His way] in ridicule ...}*" until His saying: "*{And when Our verses are recited to him, he turns away arrogantly as if he had not heard them, as if there was in his ears deafness. So, give him tidings of a painful punishment.}*" [31:6-7]. He (the Exalted) also said: "*{And those who, when reminded of the verses of their Lord, do not fall upon them deaf and blind.}*" [25:73]. He (the Exalted) also said: "*{Then what is [the matter] with them that they are, from the reminder, turning away. As if they were alarmed donkeys. Fleeing from a lion?}*" [74:49-51].

He (the Exalted) also said: "*{Indeed, the worst of living creatures in the sight of Allah are the deaf and dumb who do not use reason [i.e., the disbelievers]. Had Allah known any good in them, He would have made them hear ...}*" until the end of the verse [8:22-23]. He also said: "*{And those who disbelieve say: "Do not listen to this Qur'ān and speak noisily during [the recitation of] it that perhaps you will overcome."}*" [41:26]. He (the Exalted) also said: "*{Then what is [the matter] with them that they are, from the reminder, turning away. As if they were alarmed donkeys. Fleeing from a lion?}*" [74:49-51]. There are many such examples in the Qur'an.

This was the hearing of the early Muslims, their prominent Sheikhs and Imams such as the Companions, the Followers and the scholars who came after them, such as Ibrahim ibn Adham, al-Fudhail ibn Iyadh, abu Sulaiman al-Darany, Ma'rouf al-Karkhy, Yusuf ibn Asbat, Hudhaifah al-Mar'ashy and the likes of those.

Umar ibn al-Khattab (may Allah be pleased with him) often said to abu Moussa al-Ash'ary: "*Remind us of our Lord,*" so he recited while they listened and wept. When the Companions of Muhammad (PBUH) gathered, they used to command one of them to recite the Qur'an while the others listened. It is stated in the Sahih that the Prophet (PBUH) passed by abu Moussa al-Ash'ary while he recited, so he (PBUH) kept listening to his recitation and said: "***This man has been given a Mizmar (sweet melodious voice) among the Mazamir of the family of Dawud,*** *peace be upon him.*" He also said to him: "***I passed by you yesterday while you were reciting so I kept listening to your recitation.***" He said: "*If I had known you were listening, I would have beautified it for you even more.*" The Prophet (PBUH) also said: "***Beautify the Qur'an with your voices.***"

He also said: "***Allah listens more attentively to a man with a beautiful voice who recites Qur'an out loud than the master of a singing slave listens to his slave.***" He (PBUH) also said: "***Allah does not listen so attentively to anything as He listens to the recitation of the Qur'an by a Prophet who recites well with a melodious and audible voice.***"

He also said: "***He who does not recite the Qur'an in a melodious tone is not of us.***"

This is why listening is among the great resources and fine tastes and an increase in knowledge and significant states in a manner that no speech or book can encompass. Additionally, contemplating upon the Qur'an and understanding it increases knowledge and faith in a manner than no eloquence can contain.

One should be aware that Allah (the Exalted) said in His book: "*{Say, [O Muhammad]}*" "*If you should love Allah, then follow* *me, [so] Allah will love you ...}"* [3:31]. A group of early scholars said: *"Some people, during the Prophet's (PBUH) lifetime, claimed to love Allah, so Allah revealed this verse: "{Say, [O Muhammad], "If you should love Allah, then follow me, [so] Allah will love you ...}" until the end of the verse."* Thus, Allah (the Exalted) clarified that loving Him necessitates following the Messenger (PBUH), and that following the Messenger entails Allah's love for the servant. Such love is the trial for those who allege to love Allah, as allegations and doubts increase in this regard. It is narrated about **Dhul-Nun al-Misry**, that people talked about the issue of Love [for Allah] in front of him, so he said: *"Keep quiet about this issue, lest the people hear it and allege it."*

Some said: *"Whoever worships Allah through love alone is a heretic, whoever worships Allah through fear alone is a Haruri[20], whoever worships Him through hope alone is a Murji'[21], and whoever worships Him through love, fear and hope is a*

---

[20] A person who belongs to al-Haruriyah or al-Muhakkimah, which is an offshoot sect of the Kharijites.

[21] A person who belongs to Murji'as or Murji'ites, who hold the opinion that God alone has the right to judge whether or not a Muslim has become an apostate, and so Muslims should practice postponement ('irjā') of judgment on committers of major sins and not make charges of disbelief ('takfir') or punish accordingly anyone who has professed Islam to be their faith.

monotheist believer." This is because in mere love, the souls feel at ease until they go too far in their desires if they are not inhibited by the restraint of fear of Allah, so much so that the Jews said: "*{"We are the children of Allah and His beloved.}*" [5:18]. The allegers of love contradict the Sharia more often than the people of fear [of Allah], which is why He coupled it with fear in His saying: "*{[It will be said]: "This is what you were promised - for every returner [to Allah] and keeper [of His covenant], who feared the Most Merciful in the unseen and came with a heart returning [in repentance]. Enter it in peace. This is the Day of Eternity."}*" [50:32-34].

The scholars who wrote books about the Sunnah stated in their beliefs avoiding those who frequently proclaim love and engage therein without fear, due to what is therein of corruption, in which many groups of Sufis fell. What these people experienced of corrupt beliefs and deeds caused some groups renouncing the foundation of the Sufist way entirely, and those deviants are divided into two groups:

- A group that approves of its truth and falsehood
- A group that disapproves of its truth and falsehood, as some groups of theologians and jurists do.

The correct manner is to approve what conforms to the Book and the Sunnah therein and elsewhere, and disapprove of what contradicts the Book and the Sunnah therein and elsewhere.

Allah (the Exalted) said: "*{Say, [O Muhammad]: "If you should love Allah, then follow me, [so] Allah will love you and forgive you your sins ...}*" [3:31]. Therefore, following the Sunnah and the Sharia of the Messenger (PBUH) in secret and in openness is the reason for Allah's love, just as Jihad in His cause, allying oneself with His allies and antagonizing His enemies is its essence, as the Hadith said: "*The firmest handhold of faith is love for the sake of Allah and hatred for the sake of Allah.*" Another hadith says: "*He who loves for the sake of Allah, hates for the sake of Allah, gives for the sake of Allah and denies for the sake of Allah has completed his faith.*"

Many who allege love are farther than others from following the Sunnah, from commanding what is right and forbidding what is wrong, and from Jihad in Allah's cause, and they further allege that this is more appropriate for the path of love because they allege that the path of love has no zeal or anger for the sake of Allah, which contradicts what the Book and the Sunnah state. The transmitted hadith states: "*On the Day of Resurrection, Allah (the Exalted) will say: "Where are those who have mutual love for the sake of My Glory? Today I shall shelter them in My Shade when there will be no shade except Mine.*" His saying "Where are those who have mutual love for the sake of My Glory?" outlines what their hearts contain of glorification and veneration for Allah whist loving each other for His sake, and with that they observe His limits, rather than those who do not due to the weakness of faith in their hearts. Those are the people mentioned in the hadith [Qudsi]: "*My love is due to those who love one another for My sake, meet one another for My sake, visit one another for My sake and spend in charity for My sake.*" There are many hadiths about those who love each other for Allah's sake.

It is stated in the Sahih books, as narrated by Abu Hurairah (may Allah be pleased with him) that the Prophet (PBUH) said: "*There are seven types of people whom Allah will give Shade of His Thrown on the Day when there would be no shade other than His Throne's Shade: A just ruler; a youth who grew up worshipping Allah; a man whose heart is attached to mosque when he leaves it until he returns to it; two persons who love and meet each other and depart from each other for the sake of Allah; a man who gives in charity and conceals it (to such an extent) that the left hand does not know what the right has given; a person who remembers Allah in solitude and his eyes well up (with tears); and a man whom a woman of status and beauty seduces (for illicit relation), but he (rejects this offer by saying): "I fear Allah."*"

• CHAPTER 12 •

The Foundation of Love is Knowledge about Allah

The foundation of love is knowledge about Allah (the Exalted, the Majestic), which has two foundations:

(First): which is known as: **the love of the public** for His beneficence to His servants. Such love with such foundation is not denied by anyone, for the hearts are created in such a manner as to love whoever is kind to them and hate whoever does them hard. Allah (the Exalted) is the truly Kind Benefactor to His servant, and He is the granter of all blessings, even if they were granted through an intermediary, for He is the facilitator of intermediaries and the causer of means. However, if such love does not attract the heart to love Allah Himself, then the servant does not, in fact, love anyone except himself. Similarly, anyone who loves something for its kindness to him, does not love, in truth, except himself. Such is not criticized but praised.

This love is the one outlined by the saying of the Prophet (PBUH): "**Love Allah for what He nourishes you with of His Blessings, love me due to the love of Allah, and love the people of my house due to love of me.**" The person who limits himself to this love does not know, regarding Allah, what necessitates loving Him except His beneficence to him. This is as was said: **Praise is due to Allah in two manners:**

- "Praise": meaning gratitude, which is only for His blessing.
- And "Praise": meaning exaltation, glorification and love for Him for what He Himself deserves.

Similarly for love, the (second) foundation is loving Him for that for which He is worthy. This is the love of those who know about Allah what He deserves to be loved for. There is not an aspect for which Allah is known, which is indicated by His names and attributes, except He deserved full love for that aspect, even all His actions, as every blessing from Him is a favor, and every retribution from Him is justice. Thus, He is worthy of praise in every state, and He is worthy of praise for ease and hardship. This is higher and more perfect, and this is **the love of the select few.**

Those are the ones who seek the pleasure of gazing at His honorable face and who enjoy exalting and conversing with Him. To them, this is more vital than water for the fish, and if they were separated from that, they would experience insufferable pain, and they are the forerunners, as stated in Sahih Muslim, that Abu Hurairah (may Allah be pleased with him) said: Allah's Messenger (PBUH) happened to pass by a mountain called Jumdan. He said: "**Proceed on, it is Jumdan, Mufarradun have gone ahead.**" They said: "*Allah's Messenger, who are Mufarradun?*" He said: "**They are the men and women who remember Allah often.**" In another version, he said: "**Those who absorb themselves in the remembrance of Allah, and remembrance removed their heavy burdens from them, until they will come on the Day of Judgement being light (in weight of their burdens).**" The one who absorbs himself in the remembrance of Allah is fond of it, enjoys it and does not grow weary of it.

In the hadith narrated by Harun ibn Antrara from his father that Ibn Abbas (may Allah be pleased with them) said: "*Moses said: "O Lord! Which of Your servants is the dearest to you?" He said:

"The one who remembers Me and does not forget me." He said: *"Which of Your servants is most knowledgeable."* He said: **"He who seeks the knowledge of people in addition to his own to find a word that points him towards guidance or turns him away from ruin."** He said: *"Which of Your servants is the wisest?"* He said: *"He who rules against himself as he rules against others and rules for others as he rules for himself.""* In this hadith, he mentioned love, knowledge and wisdom, which is the combination of all good things.

One must be aware that it is not permitted to assue, with regards to Allah's love, what is assumed regarding the love of others, such as false accusation, abandonment and alienation for no reason and so on which some people might falsely assume to the extent that they liken His love to the love of those who avert and cut off without a cause or push away those who attempt to draw closer, even if some authors mistakenly write that in their writings, causing the gist of their words to establish an argument against Allah. Rather, with Allah is the conclusive argument.

It is stated in the Sahih books, as narrated by Abu Hurairah, that the Prophet (PBUH) said: ***"Allah (the Exalted) said: "If my servant remembers Me in himself, I too, remember him in***

Myself; and if he remembers Me in a group of people, I remember him in a group that is better than they; and if he comes one span nearer to Me, I go one cubit nearer to him; and if he comes one cubit nearer to Me, I go a distance of two outstretched arms nearer to him; and if he comes to Me walking, I go to him running." In some narrations, Allah (the Exalted) said: *"Those who remember Me are My companions, those who praise Me are My visitors, those who obey Me are My honored ones. As for those who disobey Me, I do not make them despair of My mercy; if they repent, I am their lover* — as Allah loves the repentant — *and if they do not repent, I am their doctor: I try them with affliction in order to purify them of defects."*

Allah (the Exalted) said: *"{But he who does of righteous deeds while he is a believer - he will neither fear injustice nor deprivation.}"* [20:112]. They said: injustice means making him bear the sins of another, and deprivation is to reduce his own good deeds. He (the Exalted) also said: *"{... And We did not wrong them [thereby], but they were wronging themselves.}"* [16:118]. It is narrated in the authentic hadith by Abu Dharr (may Allah be pleased with him) that the Prophet (PBUH) said: *"Allah (the Exalted), said: "O My servants, I have forbidden oppression for Myself and have made it forbidden amongst you, so do not oppress one another. O My servants, all of you are astray except those whom I have guided, so seek guidance of Me and I shall guide you, O My servants, all of you are hungry except those whom I have fed, so seek food of Me and I shall feed you. O My servants, all of you are naked except those whom I have clothed, so seek clothing of Me and I shall clothe you. O My servants, you sin by night and by day, and I forgive all sins, so seek forgiveness of Me and I shall forgive you. O My servants, you can neither do Me any harm nor do Me any good. O My servants, were the first of you and the last of you, the human of you and the jinn of you to be as pious as the most pious heart of any one man of you, that would not increase My dominion in the slightest. O My servants, were the first of you and the last of you, the human of you and the jinn of you to be as wicked as the most wicked heart of any one man of you, that would not decrease My dominion in the slightest. O My servants, were the first of you and the last of you, the human of you and the jinn of you to rise up in one place and make a request of Me, and were I to give everyone what he requested, that would not decrease what I have, any more than a needle decreases the sea if dipped into it. O My servants, it is but your deeds that I record for you and then recompense you for. So let him who finds good, praise Allah, and let him who finds other than that blame no one but himself."*

Similarly, what is transmitted by al-Bukhari [in his Sahih], as narrated by Shaddad ibn Aws, that the Messenger (PBUH) said: *"The best supplication for seeking forgiveness is to say: "O Allah! You are my Lord. There is no deity except You. You have created me, and I am Your slave, and I hold to Your Covenant as far as I can. I seek refuge in You from the evil of what I have done. I acknowledge the favors that You have bestowed upon me, and I confess my sins. Pardon me, for none but You has the power to pardon." If anyone says that during the day with firm belief in it and dies before the evening, he will be one of the dwellers of Paradise; and if anyone says that during the night with firm belief in it and dies before the morning, he will be one of the dwellers of Paradise."*

The servant always lies between a blessing from Allah, for which he needs praise, and a sin from him, for which he needs to seek forgiveness. Each of these is among the matters that accompany the servant at all times, for he remains surrounded by the blessings of Allah, and he remains in need for repentance and seeking forgiveness.

This is why the master of the Sons of Adam, and the leader of the pious, Muhammad (PBUH), used to ask for forgiveness in every state.

He (PBUH) said in the authentic hadith transmitted by al-Bukhari: "*O people! Repent to your Lord, for By Allah, I ask for forgiveness from Allah and turn to Him in repentance more than seventy times a day.*" It is stated in Sahih Muslim that he (PBUH) said: "*My heart is sometimes invaded by inattentiveness, and I ask God's forgiveness a hundred times a day.*" Abdullah ibn Umar said: "We used to count for the Messenger of Allah (PBUH) in the single council that he says: "*O my Lord! Forgive me and accept my repentance, for You are the Accepter of Repentance, the Merciful,*" a hundred times."

This is why it is recommended to ask forgiveness at the end of every deed. Allah (the Exalted) said: "*{... and those who seek forgiveness before dawn.}*" [3:17]. Some said: "*Spend the night in prayer,*" and when it is the time before dawn, they command seeking forgiveness. It is transmitted in the Sahih books that when the Prophet (PBUH) finished his prayed, he asked Allah for forgiveness thrice and said: "*O Allah, You are Peace and from You comes peace. Blessed are You, O Owner of majesty and honor.*" He (the Exalted) said: "*{... But when you depart* *from Arafat, remember Allah at al-Mash'ar al-Haram ...}*" until His saying: "*{... and ask forgiveness of Allah. Indeed, Allah is Forgiving and Merciful.}*" [2:198-199]. After the Prophet (PBUH) conveyed the message, strived for Allah with the striving due to Him, and did what Allah commanded Him to do, which none other could reach, Allah (the Exalted) said to him: "*{When the victory of Allah has come and the conquest, And you see the people entering into the religion of Allah in multitudes, Then exalt [Him] with praise of your Lord and ask forgiveness of Him. Indeed, He is ever Accepting of Repentance.}*" [110:1-3].

This is why the pillars of the religion are Tawhid and asking for forgiveness, as He (the Exalted) said: "*{Alif, Lām, Rā. [This is] a Book whose verses are perfected and then presented in detail from [one who is] Wise and Aware [Through a messenger, saying]: "Do not worship except Allah. Indeed, I am to you from Him a warner and a bringer of good tidings," And [saying]: "Seek forgiveness of your Lord and repent to Him, [and] He will let you enjoy a good provision ...}*" until the end of the verse [11:1-3]. He also said: "*{... so take a straight course to Him and seek His forgiveness ...}*" [41:6]. He (the Exalted) also said: "*{So know, [O Muḥammad], that there is no deity*

except Allah and ask forgiveness for your sin and for the believing men and believing women ...} " [47:19].

Moreover, the hadith states: "*Satan says: "I destroyed the people with sins, and they destroyed me with the statement: "There is no deity except Allah," and with asking forgiveness [from Allah].*"" Yunus (PBUH) said: "***{There is no deity except You; exalted are You. Indeed, I have been of the wrongdoers.}***" [21:87]. When the Prophet (PBUH) rode his mount, he used to praise Allah, utter Takbir thrice and say: "***There is no deity except you. Glory belongs to you. I have wronged myself, so forgive me.***" Moreover, Kaffarat al-Majlis (Atonement for the sins of the council), with which he used to conclude the council is: "***Glory belongs to You, O Allah, and praise belongs to You. I bear witness that there no deity except You. I seek Your forgiveness and repent to You.***"

Allah knows best, and may Allah bestow His mercy and peace upon Muhammad.

THE END

ABOUT THE AUTHOR

Taqī ad-Dīn Ahmad ibn Taymiyyah, known as Ibn Taymiyyah born in 1263 AD, one of the most Famous Muslim scholars.

Had a wide knowledge in different subject and strong views base on Islamic source and sunnah Tradition.

www.ingramcontent.com/pod-product-compliance
Lightning Source LLC
Chambersburg PA
CBHW070938180426
43192CB00039B/2320